A NEW GUIDE TO
OLD FLORIDA ATTRACTIONS

FROM MERMAIDS TO SINGING TOWERS

SECOND EDITION

Doug Alderson

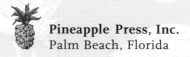

Pineapple Press, Inc.
Palm Beach, Florida

An imprint of The Rowman & Littlefield Publishing Group, Inc.
4501 Forbes Blvd., Ste. 200
Lanham, MD 20706
www.rowman.com

Distributed by NATIONAL BOOK NETWORK

[Photos: The Historical Society of Palm Beach County and Robert Yarnell Richie photographs, circa 1932–1934, DeGolyer Library, Southern Methodist University.]

British Library Cataloguing in Publication Information Available

Library of Congress Cataloging-in-Publication Data Available

Names: Alderson, Doug, author.
Title: A new guide to old Florida attractions : from mermaids to singing
   towers / Doug Alderson.
Description: [Second edition] | Palm Beach, Florida : Pineapple Press,
   Inc., [2020] | Includes bibliographical references and index. | Summary:
   "A New Guide to Old Florida Attractions, 2nd edition, takes you on an
   unforgettable journey across the Sunshine State. Discover what Florida's
   golden age of tourism was, and still is, all about—magical and
   beautiful"— Provided by publisher.
Identifiers: LCCN 2020005573 (print) | LCCN 2020005574 (ebook) | ISBN
   9781683340867 (paperback) | ISBN 9781683340874 (epub)
Subjects: LCSH: Florida—Guidebooks.
Classification: LCC F309.3 .A56 2020 (print) | LCC F309.3 (ebook) | DDC
   917.5904—dc23
LC record available at https://lccn.loc.gov/2020005573
LC ebook record available at https://lccn.loc.gov/2020005574

To all who share in the love and magic of Old Florida

CONTENTS

ACKNOWLEDGMENTS

Part of the joy of journeying through the golden age of Florida tourism has been meeting people with similar passions. Their eyes light up when you mention certain attractions and experiences, and they often share personal stories. In addition, they might point to something you have missed because the Florida tourism road map contains many layers and twists. One such helpful person has been Florida native Tracie Schneider of Tallahassee. She and her two daughters share a website (3florida girls), where they sell classic Florida souvenirs. Tracie was the first person to read a draft of this book, and she did so with enthusiasm. Her feedback was invaluable. Thank you, Tracie!

My family and close friends have been ever supportive as well, especially my dear wife, Cyndi. She gives me space when I need it, helps me lug books to promotional events, and laughs at the right moments during presentations. I am indeed fortunate. A writer's life can be lonely at times, but her warm face and many others are there to greet me when I emerge from my cocoon.

I'd also like to thank the folks at Pineapple Press. I've always enjoyed working with them and appreciate their efforts to maintain quality, distribute my books, and keep retail prices reasonable.

Taking in the sights in Florida postcard, circa 1906.

Published by H. & W. B. Drew Company, Jacksonville

PREFACE

Florida. We didn't know what to expect, but images of palm trees and white sand beaches filled our heads as we packed our old Rambler station wagon with luggage for six people—Mom, Dad, Grandma, my two brothers, and me. Snow had recently melted away in our Illinois yard as we embarked on our first trip to the Sunshine State in 1966.

When we reached our first welcome station at the Florida border, my brothers and I were afflicted with advanced cases of tourist fever. We collected stacks of brochures for various attractions and begged our parents to stop at all of them. Tops on the list were Silver Springs and the giant snakes found at the Ross Allen Reptile Institute; Six Gun Territory, where Old West shootouts occurred daily; and the alluring mermaids of Weeki Wachee Springs.

We traveled Highway 19 through the spine of Florida toward my aunt's house in Largo, stopping at a decrepit and disappointing zoo just south of Perry, with cramped concrete quarters for bears and other animals. Due to time and budget constraints, we avoided most of the major tourist attractions, although my parents did allow me to buy a large coconut carved in the likeness of a tiki god, a stuffed baby alligator (live ones were no longer sold), and other kitschy souvenirs. My parents geared our visits to places that were relatively inexpensive, especially those that had an educational component. One stop was the Ringling Museum in Sarasota, a stopover still worth the effort today because it features outstanding artwork from world masters as well as a circus museum. Edison's Winter Estate in Fort Myers was as interesting then as it is now, but one of our stops won't be matched anytime soon. It was a replica of the HMS *Bounty* sailing ship in St. Petersburg, the vessel used in the classic 1962 film *Mutiny on the Bounty*, starring Marlon Brando. My brothers and I were able to man the cannons and pretend to be real Old World sailors and pirates. Sadly, Hurricane Sandy sank the ship in October 2012 while it was sailing toward its winter home in St. Petersburg from New London, Connecticut.

FLORIDA "SOUTHERN EXPOSURE"

Southern exposure postcard, circa 1940.

Two years after our first visit to Florida, my family moved to Tallahassee, where Dad got a job teaching at Florida State University. Suddenly Florida was our backyard. We visited Marineland along the east coast, the Everglades and the keys, and most of the major state parks that existed then. Over time, we noticed that interstate travel was becoming more of the norm, quickening the pace of Sunshine State driving. Plus, a little mouse in Orlando was changing the face of Florida tourism. Mega theme parks were becoming the main draws, and many of Florida's original tourism attractions were being relegated to the sidelines or else fading into memory.

In 2014, I joined my friend Liz Sparks in kayaking scenic side channels through the new Silver Springs State Park. The water was clear, turtles sunned on logs, and a large bull alligator bellowed just ahead of us. This was natural Florida at its finest. Then we started gliding past ruins of a Seminole village, a pioneer camp, and a large log fort, all once part of the vast offerings that had made Silver Springs one of the top tourist attractions in Florida during its heyday. We began to list some of the other Old Florida attractions (most of them springs) that are now part of Florida's award-winning state park system: Wakulla, Homosassa, Weeki Wachee, De Leon, and Rainbow. Plus, other Old Florida tourist mainstays were still holding on, such as Bok Tower near Lake Wales, the St. Augustine Alligator Farm, and Sunken Gardens in St. Petersburg. And I was aware of relatively newer attractions that seemed equally intriguing, such as Solomon's Castle in central Florida and tarpon feeding at Robbie's of Islamorada in the keys.

On our way back to Tallahassee from Silver Springs, Liz and I drove north on Highway 301, one of the early tourist routes through the peninsula. We stopped at a fruit stand, toured the historical Marjorie Kinnan Rawlings Historic State Park in Cross Creek, and ate venison and catfish at the Yearling Restaurant while listening to blues sung by an aged performer named Willie Green. I felt alive with the way Florida used to be—and still is, in places. That's when my quest to find more of "Lost Florida" accelerated.

When I returned home, I looked through my mail and perused a collection of vintage Wakulla Springs postcards I had purchased on eBay. The oldest card was from the late 1930s, and on the back was one large signature: Johnny Weissmuller. Based on online examples, it seemed authentic. Weissmuller was a former Olympic swimmer and the most famous of the Tarzan actors. In 1941, he was featured in parts of two movies filmed at Wakulla Springs—*Tarzan's Secret Treasure* and *Tarzan's New York Adventure*. I assume someone got his autograph

Liz Sparks beside the Yearling Restaurant sign.

Doug Alderson

Inside the Yearling Restaurant.

Doug Alderson

A Glass-bottom Boat and Bathing Floats
WAKULLA SPRINGS, FLORIDA
The Largest and Deepest Spring in the World
Noted for its Pole Vaulting Fish and many
other varieties of Tropical Fish
Ideal Bathing Resort
Water Temperature 71 degrees the year 'round

PUBLISHED BY WAKULLA SPRINGS, INC., WAKULLA, FLORIDA

HANDCOLORED
POST CARD

THE FINEST AMERICAN MADE VIEW POST CARDS—THE ALBERTYPE CO., BROOKLYN, N.Y.

Early Wakulla Springs postcard with Johnny Weissmuller's signature on the back.

there during filming, especially since several locals served as extras for the movies and Weissmuller was known for being generous with his signature. It seemed a confirmation of my quest. And now I invite you to share the journey with me.

A FLORIDA WITCHES' BREW

To create an Old Florida style roadside attraction,
Start with a cauldron of cool Silver Springs water.
Add camellia petals from Maclay Gardens,
Hair from a Weeki Wachee mermaid,
An alligator tooth from Gatorland,
And a blank bullet from Six Gun Territory.
Infuse the brew with the vibration of Bok Tower bells,
A Seminole stomp dance,
Screams from a Miracle Strip roller coaster,
And a Johnny Weissmuller Tarzan yell.
Stir in a handful of Emerald Coast beach sand,
A brick from St. Augustine's oldest house,
Beer from Sloppy Joe's,
And spray from a Marineland dolphin.
Mix thoroughly with a dose of Ross Allen entrepreneurship,
A dose of hucksterism,
And a sprinkle of good fortune.
Bake in the Florida sun,
Pray for a cold northern winter,
And watch it grow.

PART I

FLORIDA TOURISM
THROUGH THE AGES

ONE

Early Tourists and Healing Waters

◇◇◇◇◇◇◇◇◇◇◇◇◇◇◇◇◇◇

"We have done it! Whether in the body or not, we have been to dream-land, to the land of the fays and the elves, the land where reality ceases and romance begins."

Harriet Beecher Stowe, *1873, writing about a steamboat trip to Silver Springs*

Surely Native Americans were the first Florida tourists. Humans being humans, they sought the beautiful and unusual as well as adventure and good food: "Hey, I hear there's a huge spring full of catfish at Standing Eagle's camp. Let's go pay him a visit." "They make the best corn soup at Mud Turtle's village. Why don't we swing by on the way to your mother's?" "Brave Seeker's camp on the big river has a dugout that fits fifteen people! He takes it on long voyages to far-off lands and gets the most unusual trade items."

Of course, these are hypothetical situations, but any people who had occupied a land for more than fourteen thousand years would have known it well and enjoyed visiting special places and people. The natural world was the number one theme park then—no exotic zoos, gardens, or kitschy shows—

and in pre-Columbian Florida, that was enough. Florida was named *la Florida* (the land of flowers) by early Spanish visitors for a reason. It was a subtropical Eden. Dangerous if you were careless, but breathtakingly beautiful and unique.

The Seminoles knew it. That's why they hung on so tenaciously in the deep swamps rather than be shipped to lands in the West. Florida was home. Unsurpassed.

One could argue that early Europeans who landed on Florida's shores were tourists. Some certainly were, seeking new sights and sounds—adventure! Others primarily sought riches, land, and domination, and so a centuries-long conflict ensued. It can be difficult to revel in the beauty of a spring or a beach when people are shooting arrows at you. Just ask Alvar

Núñez Cabeza de Vaca, that hapless Spaniard who had joined Pánfilo de Narváez on an ill-fated tour of North Florida in 1528. His epic tale of grim survival at the hands of native people and the elements did little to promote the Sunshine State.

"We felt certain we would all be stricken," he wrote of being trapped along Apalachee Bay while they waited for ships that never came, "with death the one foreseeable way out; and in such a place, death seemed all the more terrible." With few tools, materials, or carpentry skills, the crew built five crude sailing vessels for the 242 survivors to sail west. After six thousand miles in eight years, only four men straggled into Mexico City.

After de Vaca's story became known and his journal was published, it's a wonder anyone else wanted to explore Florida, but they did.

After more tales of woe (such as Jonathan Dickinson's gripping account of being captured by Indians and walking half-starved to St. Augustine), the stories of Florida began to change. The writings of William Bartram in the late 1700s, for example, stirred the imaginations of a young country and Europe. Bartram was a naturalist who marveled at the biodiversity, wild beauty, and native peoples of Florida in the late 1700s. Here's Bartram's account of crossing Paynes Prairie near present-day Gainesville:

> Next day we passed over part of the great and beautiful Alachua Savanna, whose exuberant green meadows, with the fertile hills which immediately encircle it, would, if peopled and cultivated after the manner of the civilized countries of Europe, without crowding or incommoding families, at the moderate estimation, accommodate in the happiest manner above one hundred thousand human inhabitants, besides millions of domestic animals; and I make no doubt this place will at some future day be one of the most populous and delightful seats on earth.

No other eighteenth-century advertisement to visit and settle Florida could have done a better job, and it proved prophetic. The current population of Gainesville, a popular university city, hovers around 134,000.

John James Audubon, in the 1830s, attributed an early land boom to Bartram's flowery prose, and Bartram inspired several romanticist poets and writers of the era. But Audubon believed that reality did not always match Bartram's prose. "When the United States purchased the peninsula from the Spanish Government," he wrote, "the representations given of it by Mr. Bartram and other poetical writers were soon found greatly to exceed the reality. For this reason, many of the individuals who flocked to it, returned home or made their way towards other regions with a heavy heart; yet the climate during the winter months is the most delightful that could be imagined."

The first edition of William Bartram's Travels through North and South Carolina, Georgia, East and West Florida, *photographed in the Maclay House in Tallahassee.*

Doug Alderson

In one letter, Audubon referred to Bartram after visiting an island in the St. Johns River covered with sour orange trees: "Mr. Bartram was the first to call this a garden, but he is to be forgiven; he was an enthusiastic botanist, and rare plants, in the eyes of such a man, convert a wilderness at once into a garden." Ironically, Audubon's party named the place "Audubon Island."

As the Second Seminole War began to wind down, part of Major Henry Whiting's diary was published in a journal in 1839. His words about Florida's north-flowing St. Johns River— what some would later call "the American Nile"—proved prophetic: "Invalids have long looked to Florida as a refuge from the Northern winter, and during the disturbances of the last few years, St. Augustine has necessarily been the only place of resort. But when peace

shall be established and the St. Johns reoccupied, that river will present many places of great attraction to the infirm and pulmonic."

After the Seminole Wars and Civil War were put to rest, Florida's tourist trade began to kick in, especially during the winter months. Southerners came up with a humorous phrase that rang true: "A Yankee tourist is worth a bale of cotton, and twice as easy to pick."

From Jacksonville's luxury hotels, steamboats began bringing tourists up a maze of rivers, most notably the St. Johns and Ocklawaha. "The shores of the St. John's are wanting in what forms the great beauty of the Hudson—the hills and mountains, to enhance the grandeur of the landscape," states the 1875 *Guide to Florida* by "Rambler." "Here the banks seldom

SILVER SPRING.

1882 Silver Springs illustration.

rise more than twenty feet above its placid waters. The scene is, however, most picturesque; and, as the steamer glides over the mirror-like surface, the passengers are loud in their expressions of admiration. From time to time groves of orange trees, covered with golden fruit, are passed—the contrast between them and the forests of oak, pine and cypress, which fringe the shores, making an agreeable variety."

Freshwater springs were front and center for many steamboat excursions, especially the azure depths of Silver Springs. A *Harper's Magazine* article in the 1880s boosted interest, and a hotel was built on the shore of the main spring. A railroad and stagecoach line soon connected to it as well. Then someone figured out a way to put glass in the bottom of a boat, and a profitable enterprise was born. Notable dignitaries to visit Silver Springs included poet Sidney Lanier, writer Harriet Beecher Stowe, inventor Thomas Edison, and Northern Civil War leaders Ulysses S. Grant and William Tecumseh Sherman.

Journalist George M. Barbour accompanied Ulysses Grant on an all-night steamboat trip up the Ocklawaha to the spring in 1880. "These covered passages are solemn and impressive at any time; but in the night, when lighted up by the blaze of the brilliant

THE ILLUMINATED OCKLAWAHA FOREST.
A WEIRDLY BEAUTIFUL RADIANCE.

Postcard photo of the steamboat Hiawatha *making its way up the Ocklawaha River, postmarked 1917.*

bonfire burning on the roof of the wheel-house, then the scene is quite indescribable," he wrote in *Florida for Tourists, Invalids, and Settlers.* "The inky water, the lights and shadows of the foliage, the disturbed birds as they wheel gracefully out of sight, all leave an impression never to be forgotten."

Barbour also had kind words to say about the people of Tallahassee, Florida's capital, as evidenced by the testimonial in the front of his book by then governor W. D. Bloxham, former governor George F. Drew, and two other high-ranking officials: "Nowhere, it may be said in conclusion, is there a more refined and cultured society than in Tallahassee. Among them are many descendants of the most prominent and aristocratic old families of America."

But of Wakulla County, just to the south, Barbour wrote,

In Wakulla County is a vast jungle of trees, vines, water, and marsh, that has never yet been fully explored. . . . Several adventurous gentlemen in Tallahassee have, on various occasions, attempted to penetrate its depths, but found it impossible except at much expense. As far as they penetrated, they found a strange country of volcanic appearance. Everywhere were seen great masses of rocks, often an acre in extent, all cracked and ragged as if upheaved from a great depth. . . . It is in this impenetrable jungle that the famous "Florida volcano" is supposed to exist, for a column of light, hazy smoke or vapor may be (and has been for years) seen rising from some portion of it, and provokes the conundrum, "What is it?"

The smoke plume from the "Wakulla Volcano" that baffled both residents and visitors alike for decades suddenly disappeared forever after the Charleston earthquake of 1886. It was one more mysterious phenomenon to add to the Florida mystique. Whether it was due to a peat fire, a natural gas vent, or some other source remains the subject of conjecture to this day.

Despite Wakulla County's near impenetrability at the time, various rail and steamboat routes allowed tourists to find numerous ways to explore Florida, including the remoter parts of Northwest Florida. "Pleasant excursion parties are sometimes made up in the spring at Columbus [Georgia]," wrote Sidney Lanier in 1875, "for the purpose of descending the Chattahoochee and Apalachicola in a chartered steamer, fishing, hunting, and exploring the strange Dead Lakes of Calhoun County, as well as the brighter waters of St. Josephs, St. Andrews, and other beautiful bays of this coast."

Tales of Florida's abundant and unusual wildlife, such as the alligator, drew sportsmen from throughout the country, and there were no conservation laws to limit wanton killing. Rambler's 1875 Florida guide was highly subsidized by steamboat lines and motels, and Florida was made to sound like a boundless Eden for the sports-man: "It is during the cold season, when the northern sportsmen are confined indoors, that the game is most plentiful in Florida. Deer, bear, wild cat, raccoon, 'possum, wild turkey, ducks, geese, snipe, woodcock, quails, partridge, and curlews, are plentiful, and offer fine hunting; while the rivers, bays, and lakes, invite the stranger to the pleasures of the rod, filled as they are with schools of the finest fish."

Surprisingly, Rambler's guide—near the back—offered an alarming note with regard to Florida's roseate spoonbills, often referred to as "pink curlews" during the period: "This rare bird, however, is nearly exterminated. Their skins bring from ten to twenty dollars. Their roosts are ruthlessly destroyed, and they are shot without regard to time or condition. They lay but two eggs, and no opportunity for increase is afforded. Numbers are killed and thrown aside because of imperfections. During Sir Francis Sykes' visit to Indian River he sent to England one hundred and sixty-eight perfect roseate spoonbills, but it is calculated that he shot over five hundred to secure the number." Many other wading bird populations would soon be similarly decimated for their plumes, and colorful species such as ivory-billed woodpeckers and Carolina parakeets would be rendered extinct, a downfall partly attributed to the desires of early Florida tourists and visiting collectors.

James A. Henshall, in *Camping and Cruising in Florida* (published in 1884), bragged about Florida's Gulf Coast south of Cedar Key: "The Gulf coast of Florida is, perhaps, the finest cruising ground for small yachts in the world. The water is shallow, and seldom rough, for it takes a gale of wind to kick up much of a sea, and harbors lie plentifully all along the coast. Small boats can find an inside passage from Cedar Key to Cape Sable, almost the entire distance. . . . My pen is inadequate to describe the pleasures to be enjoyed, and the beauties and wonders of nature to be observed, during a winter spent on the southern coasts of Florida."

Foreign visitors likewise extolled the virtues of Florida, which brought more Europeans to explore the Sunshine State. In 1895, the Frenchman Paul Bourget wrote *Outre-Mer: Impressions of America*. In Lake Worth, near the end of his journey, he wrote, "What a country to be happy in, after

the manner of a plant that grows in the sun, unmindful and without desire to be elsewhere! . . . A warm odor and a sense of growth which inebriates, exhales from these trees and from these grasses, from these fields of pineapples, and forests of cocoanut trees."

Riding the crest of a wave in Florida tourism in the 1800s was the promise that Florida's climate and mineral springs could cure various types of ailments. People came from all over, seeking healing and respite and creating a "medical tourism" industry in the process: Soak in the waters, drink the waters—tolerating a strong sulfur taste and odor—and you'll feel better than when you first arrived. That was the hope, anyhow. Bottles and jugs of the healing liquid were brought back home by the caseload to help see one through until the next visit.

Early postcard of a winter camp in Florida, circa 1910.

Published by M. Mark, Jacksonville

Health spas opened primarily at sulfur springs, where the "rotten egg"–smelling waters were said to cure rheumatism, indigestion, dyspepsia, gastritis, syphilis, jaundice, skin diseases, and stomach, kidney, and bladder problems. More than one promoter claimed a particular spring was the original "Fountain of Youth" sought by Spanish explorer Ponce de León. The spas and adjoining hotels included the Panacea Mineral Springs along the Big Bend Gulf Coast, Newport Springs on the St. Marks River, Hampton Springs on the Fenholloway River, Suwannee Springs and White Sulphur Springs along the Suwannee River, Worthington Springs on the Santa Fe River, Green Cove Springs on the St. Johns, Orange Springs on the Ocklawaha, and Espiritu Santo Springs in Safety Harbor. Only Espiritu Santo Springs still operates as a spa today, although a late arrival to the spring/spa world, Warm Mineral Springs near Sarasota, operates as well.

Most mineral spring attractions had large hotels for overnight guests and bathhouses, benches, and concrete weir dams circling the springs, commonly known as springhouses. Testimonials of healing results from visitors were commonplace as the resorts vied for customers.

"Suwannee Springs, not far from Live Oak, is one of the most famous springs of Florida," wrote Nevin O. Winter in 1918. "It is noted for its healing qualities, while the river itself is most charming with its wooded banks."

Local historians believe Native Americans regarded White Sulphur Springs along the Suwannee River as sacred and a neutral zone, much like

Suwannee Springs as seen around 1908 in this vintage postcard photo.

Published by Valentine and Sons, New York, and printed in Great Britain

Suwannee Springs today, showing ruins of the old springhouse.

the catlinite quarries for Native American medicine pipes in southern Minnesota. It is believed that a member of any tribe could bathe in the healing waters along the Suwannee without fear of being attacked, and wounded warriors would take advantage of this refuge. According to the WPA's 1939 Florida Guide, Native Americans marked trees in a five-mile circle around the springs, and the area was also known as "Rebel's Refuge" during the Civil War since many plantation owners lived there in relative peace throughout the conflict.

White Sulphur Springs was the first Florida mineral spring to be commercialized, prompting today's promoters to call it "Florida's first tourist attraction." It was initially featured as Jackson Springs in 1831. A log cabin springhouse was built, followed by a concrete and coquina structure in 1903. The spring attraction gave rise to the town, and by the 1880s visitors could choose from five hundred hotel and boardinghouse rooms.

Green Cove Springs on the St. Johns River was known as "the Parlor City," and besides being a famous port city, it was famous for its sulfur springs. "The location of the town is very attractive, circling about a wooded and picturesque hollow, from which gushes a bold, magnificent sulphur spring, with a basin as large as the foundation of a cottage, and as deep in places as the cottage's peaked roof," wrote J. W. White in his 1890 guidebook. "The water is strong sulphur and

Interior View of the Spring House White Springs, Fla.

No publisher listed

Above: Early-nineteenth-century postcard showing the springhouse at White Springs (now called White Sulphur Springs) along the Suwannee River.

Right: Reconstructed White Springs springhouse, photographed in 2015.

Doug Alderson

The historical Adams Country Store in downtown White Springs, established in 1885, was in business during the peak of the White Springs resort.

Doug Alderson

is esteemed a very fine remedial agent in cases of neuralgia, nervous prostration, rheumatism, liver and kidney complaints. The water empties from the spring into several bathing pools of unusual size and beauty, which are open and in use all year round."

The town of Panacea was founded around several small sulfuric springs in the late 1800s. Formerly called Smith Springs, the town was renamed "Panacea"—Greek for "healing all"—to sound more appealing to visitors, a trick that seemed to work. The 125-guest Panacea Hotel was built to house the numerous visitors who came to bathe in the waters.

Hampton Springs near Perry featured the massive wooden Hotel Hampton and guaranteed its spring water as effective treatment for skin diseases, rheumatism, indigestion, dyspepsia, gastritis, and various other stomach, kidney, and bladder troubles. It was purchased by Joe Hampton before the Civil War for $10. He had been directed there by a Native American medicine man, who said the spring would aid Hampton's rheumatism and other ills. The advice proved helpful. A 1930 guidebook, *Florida, Empire of the Sun* (published by the Florida State Hotel Commission), called the attraction "a delightful resort with a club house, and a splendid mineral spring. Golfing, tennis, horseback riding and other sports are available. Hunting and fishing in the virgin wilderness, through which flows the rock-ribbed Fenholloway River, attracts many a sportsman." Theodore Roosevelt, one of the country's most famous sportsmen, was said to have been a guest.

By the mid-1930s, as roads and railroads extended deeper into the Florida peninsula, tourists began to head farther south. During the Great Depression, most mineral spring resorts became relics of the past, and many of the old hotels burned down. Some springs, such as White Sulphur Springs on the Suwannee, diminished in flow due to aquifer pumping in the region for farming, phosphate mining, and the growing city of Jacksonville to the east.

On a recent visit to Newport Springs, I waded into the cool, clear water that bore a sharp odor of hydrogen sulfide. "I guess this is what you would call a sulfur spring," I said to a man with his grandkids.

"This ain't no sulfur spring," he said. "This is stinky water!"

Still, it felt good, although there was no miraculous cure for my sore shoulder. I guess I needed to stay a few days, bring some of the "stinky water" home, and maybe drink it by the gallon. I vowed to search for another cure.

Florida's numerous freshwater lakes were also popular with visitors for bathing. A 1913 postcard showed bathers and canoeists on a lake near St. Cloud. The note on the back, written in January to a Pennsylvania friend, was typical of those from many visitors: "Hitch up your auto and come down here and take a bath. Fine weather." It was signed Amos Kiehl. An inter-

Vintage postcard, with a 1911 postmark, of a train traveling through orange groves. Most early Florida tourists traveled by train and steamboat.

Postcard published by H. & W. B. Drew Company, Jacksonville, and printed in Germany

Early postcard showing bathers in a freshwater lake at St. Cloud in 1912.

Bathing Scene, St. Cloud, Fla., Xmas, 1912.

Published by the Seminole Pharmacy and Dale's Variety Store in St. Cloud

net search revealed that Kiehl was a well-known Pennsylvania Civil War veteran. He served from 1862 to the war's end and fought in several major battles. One can only wonder what joy and solace winters in Florida may have provided during his senior years, and over the decades to come Kiehl's invitation to northern friends and relatives would be duplicated a millionfold by subsequent "snowbird" visitors.

TWO

Beaches, Highways, and a Golden Age

◇◇◇◇◇◇◇◇◇◇◇◇◇◇◇◇

Florida's coastal beaches were always popular with tourists, which is one reason why the first rail lines ran along both the Gulf and the Atlantic coasts. And beaches continue to be Florida's number one outdoor attraction.

Even automobile races were held on some beaches, such as at Daytona, made famous when Italian-born Ralph DePalma broke a world record in 1919, driving almost 150 miles per hour when most cars on the highway barely reached a third of that speed. "And what a beach!" began John Faris in his 1921 travel book, *Seeing the Sunny South.*

> *Five hundred feet wide at low tide, sloping so gently toward the water that it looks almost a plain, sand so hard-packed that the wheels of the flying automobile would leave no trace but for the weight that drives the moisture from below.*

Surf bathing in Florida postcard postmarked 1906.

Published by Asheville Postcard Company, Asheville, North Carolina

Early postcard of autos speeding along Daytona Beach with biplane, circa 1920.

There is no place like this for pleasure driving, no race-course equal to it for the annual races where world's records have been made by DePalma and Oldfield and other demons of the road.

DePalma may have found pleasure in making his mile in twenty-five seconds on the hard sands of the eighteen-mile beach, but thousands of machine-owners who are not speed maniacs have pleasure far greater in driving where it is perfectly safe to let both hands drop for a moment from the steering wheel.

Besides beaches and waters, early tourists were intrigued by Florida's surviving native inhabitants—Seminole Indians. When parts of South Florida were being developed and the Everglades drained, wild game became less abundant, and the Seminoles began to develop tourist villages so they could survive in the white man's world. Seminoles found they could retain much of their culture while making money on curious visitors who walked through their camps.

The first tourist villages were in the Miami area, easily accessed by the East Coast Railway after 1896. They included Musa Isle Indian Village, Coppinger's Tropical Gardens, Osceola's Gardens, Osceola's Indian Village, Alligator Joe's, and Tropical Hobbyland. Most camp promoters sought ways to excite the masses, and they struck Florida gold in alligator wrestling.

Seminole hunters were accustomed to the ways of the alligator, sometimes capturing the animals alive in the wild and bringing them back to their villages so the meat would stay fresh.

They also extensively hunted alligators for their skins, often used for trade at various posts. But to "wrestle" an alligator for show, Seminole men learned classic maneuvers from a white camp promoter, Henry Coppinger Jr., who had been inspired by another white man, Warren Frazee, who called himself "Alligator Joe." Beginning in 1895, Alligator Joe had dammed up creeks in South Florida to make alligator pens, and within a few years his alligator shows had become extremely popular with tourists. Coppinger taught alligator-wrestling techniques to Seminoles at his camp because he felt tourists would think it looked more authentic, and his assumption proved correct. Alligator wrestling spread through the Seminole tourist camps.

Classic maneuvers included the wrestler opening the alligator's jaw and sticking his head inside and holding an alligator's jaw shut with his chin. Tourists showed their appreciation by showering the wrestler with tips. A single show to a large, appreciative audience could net a wrestler the equivalent of a week's worth of wages from a more conventional job.

Aspects of Seminole culture put on display at villages included the Seminole wedding ceremony. A few select young couples were married several times over, all for the benefit of tourists! A Seminole craft industry also flourished, especially dolls, baskets, wood carvings, and clothing. Seminole women developed their trademark patchwork clothing, and the various

Published by H. & W. B. Drew Company, Jacksonville, and printed in Germany

Postcard of White Tiger wrestling an alligator, South Beach Alligator Farm in Florida, postmarked 1911.

Published by Pictorial Centre, Miami

Seminole wedding for tourists in Miami. Some couples were married several times in these popular public ceremonies.

designs with their symbolic meanings became popular with tourists.

The Miami area drew tourists for other reasons besides Seminoles, as aptly described by John Faris in 1921:

> One of Miami's chief attractions to the tourist is that it is possible to stay there weeks and even months without weariness, because there are so many things to do. He can stroll under the trees of the cocoanut grove near the Royal Palm Hotel, looking out on the harbor and through the cut made by the Government in the open Atlantic. That view is restful by day, but at night, when the moonlight falls on the water, it is a scene to be remembered always. A short walk will take him to the Point View residence district, where the palm-embowered houses cluster along the crescent-shaped shore of Biscayne Bay. From here the road leads to Cocoanut Grove, five miles away—five miles of riotous beauty.

Faris goes on to describe the "country home" of William Jennings Bryan near Coconut Grove, the James Deering estate—"almost hidden by festoons of bloom"—and the house of novelist Kirk Munroe, "who built his house beside Biscayne's waters before Miami made its beginning." Faris saves his best for Miami Beach: "Once an uninviting tangle, now an enchanted garden that stretches away to the north for miles. There a separate community has been built up, with residences whose gardens are like parks, hotels where wise tourists are

Published by J. N. Chamberlain, Miami

Postcard of biplane and boat racing in Miami, circa 1920.

learning to go, bathing establishments which are gateways to a beach that is remarkable even for the East Coast of Florida. Think of bathing within three miles of the Gulf Stream! . . . And this is but the beginning of the rich offerings of the Magic City."

Tourists once reached Miami chiefly by boat and then by train when Henry Flagler's East Coast Railway pushed through in 1896. Residents incorporated the city that same year and tried to rename it "Flagler," but the railroad magnate declined the honor. Even though Flagler had spent $18 million on the Florida railway to Homestead, another $20 million on the Key West extension, and $12 million for hotels along the route, "Flagler spent money for the sheer love of creating," according to J. E. Dovell in an article from the 1953 *Florida Handbook*. "The

spectacular hotels and the romantic, but ephemeral, overseas railroad were transient contributions; Flagler's abiding contribution was in the opening of the east coast wilderness to millions of latter-day discoverers of the peninsula state, many of whom have found a place in the sun and have remained to work and to play in the land of a mythical fountain of youth."

Key West was perhaps Florida's most exotic location to visit, and, like Miami, it was accessible at first only by boat and then by train when Flagler's railroad reached its final destination in 1912. Promoters boasted that the city had never experienced a frost. Charles Donald Fox, in his 1925 guidebook *The Truth about Florida*, used several glowing pages to heap praise upon Key West, best summarized by this passage: "Key West, America's Gibraltar,

Published by Detroit Publishing Company

Vintage postcard depicting Flagler's Over-Sea Railroad at the Long Key Viaduct.

Mr. H. M. Flagler's arrival with First Train
to enter Key West, Fla.

Copyright 1912 by Harris.

Published by Curt Teich & Company, Jacksonville

Postcard image of Henry Flagler fulfilling his dream as he arrives in Key West by train in 1912.

the southernmost city in the United States, and important army and navy base, has a charm and atmosphere all its own. For it is located on an island surrounded by semi-tropical depths and shoals that reproduce every color in the rainbow and whose marvelous hues and shades rival those of the Grand Canyon of Arizona. It is, perhaps, the quaintest city in the western hemisphere, and were the visitor not connected by railroad within 48 hours of New York or Chicago, he could well imagine himself in some far away and distant clime."

With the advent of the automobile in the twentieth century, more people of various income levels could explore the Sunshine State. An emerging federal highway system began to reach into Florida with north–south roads such as the Dixie Highway. By the mid-1920s, Florida had built almost nine hundred miles of hard-surfaced highways, and this number increased to more than three thousand miles by 1930, benefiting residents and farmers as well as tourists. Miami Beach real-estate developer Carl Fisher was considered the father of the Dixie Highway, and he benefited because the routes linked his developments to the broader automobile population.

The Dixie Highway (constructed from 1915 to 1927) ran from Sault Ste. Marie, Michigan, to Fisher's Miami Beach. Two parallel branches, one to the west and the other to the east, were created. The Old Spanish Trail, running from San Diego to St. Augustine, was completed in the 1920s. In Florida, the route primarily followed what today is U.S. 90. A five-mile brick section, completed in 1921 near Milton in

Published by H. & W. B. Drew Company, Jacksonville

Vintage postcard of early car crossing a Florida river.

Doug Alderson

A five-mile brick section of the Old Spanish Trail highway survives near Milton in the Florida Panhandle.

the Florida Panhandle, survives today as a bicycle and pedestrian trail paralleling U.S. 90.

As more highways were built, they received uniform numbers instead of names, with north–south routes bearing odd numbers and east–west routes even numbers. U.S. 1 largely followed the eastern branch of the Dixie Highway in Florida, with many coastal towns still having an "Old Dixie Highway" route running parallel to U.S. 1 a block or two away. Some of the original brick portions of the Dixie Highway still exist in Flagler and St. Johns Counties. The western branch of the Dixie Highway was replaced by several numbered highways: U.S. 19, 441, 17, and 41. Not surprisingly, most of the

early tourist attractions were established on these routes. U.S. 90 (the Old Spanish Trail), State Road 70, and the Tamiami Trail (U.S. 41) were the earliest east–west highways through the state. And the Overseas Highway to Key West opened in 1938 upon the demise of Flagler's railroad.

John Faris compared road and railroad travel in 1921:

> There is abundant variety for those who would travel by rail, and fortunate is the traveler who can wander first along one line, and then can choose another and another and yet another. He may take so many of them that he will be apt to think he has really seen the Sunny South by rail. He'll

find his error when he makes a study of the roads he hasn't been able to take. . . . What a contrast the automobile is! It is so easy going. You can see up, down, and around, and not simply through a narrow window. If the mood takes you, you can go up a side road. You can loiter or you can hurry on. You can see a house, a tree, an orchard, a garden or anything you want. The car is so human.

As automobile travel became more popular, a new form of tourist came on the scene—the "tin can tourist." The name may have been derived from the "Tin Lizzie" name for early automobiles, the tinned food that was often eaten on the road, or the large cans used for gasoline, water, and other liquids. With inexpensive hotels and motels in short supply during the early 1920s, tin can tourists often had homemade camper vehicles with sleeping quarters and a tiny kitchen, or they attached tents to their vehicles for sleeping. Surplus canvas military tents were popular. Barrels of water were carried to remoter areas. By the mid-1920s, small camping trailers were often pulled behind the vehicles.

The late Patrick Smith, author of *A Land Remembered* and other noteworthy Florida novels, visited Florida as a boy in 1933 on a three-week family driving trip. This is how he described it in a 2005 video interview recorded by his son:

Back then we didn't have no Holiday Inns. Instead, they had these things called tourist courts. They were little wooden cabins that rented from one-fifty to two dollars a night. And inside each

Florida "tin canners" postcard, postmarked 1924.

one of them was a little cook stove and table and chairs. I don't think we ate five meals in restaurants the whole time we were in Florida. The roads were lined solid with such things as oranges, papaya, mango, guava, and avocado. If you wanted something to eat, you parked your car and helped yourself. Back then, too, the streams that ran along the roads were so clean and filled with fish, if you wanted a fish for lunch or dinner, you parked your car and caught a grasshopper, put it on the hook and threw it in, and jerked out what you wanted to eat.

We started this trip in Pensacola. South of Pensacola we found a beautiful inlet, but we couldn't spend the night there because there was no tourist court. We passed a little country store called Destin and we passed mile after mile of uninhabited beaches with sand so white it looked like powdered sugar. It was nothing back then to drive 40, 50, 60 miles of Florida beach and see not one sign of civilization. We drove into St. Petersburg at a time when shuffleboard courts outnumbered people. We kept driving south and drove into Ft. Myers and saw those stately royal palm trees. . . . We kept driving until we came to a fishing village called Naples, then went on the old Tamiami Trail and entered Big Cypress Swamp. It was like leaving this earth and going to another planet. It was the

most beautiful, exotic place I'd ever seen.

It was nothing back then to see a native Florida panther cross in front of you. . . . When we entered the Everglades, the flights of birds overhead were so thick they actually blocked out the sun and cast shadows over land.

According to Smith, Florida was largely a wilderness when most of the country had been settled, and as late as 1937, "cow hunters" could drive a herd of cattle from Fort Pierce along the east coast to Fort Myers on the west coast and not be hindered by a fence. "Florida was the last frontier," he concluded. Florida required ranchers to fence their cattle in 1949, thus ending a colorful era in which South Florida resembled the Old West in terms of cattle drives, range wars, and crusty characters on horseback. Some Florida cowboys were even immortalized by the famous western painter Frederick Remington.

For automobile tourists, motels and "tourist courts" became more widespread and affordable in the 1930s. Wealthy tourists, however, continued to enjoy luxury hotels, primarily in coastal areas, along with activities such as horse racing, polo, and yachting.

In 1919, Tin Can Tourists of the World (TCT) formed in Tampa Bay's De Soto Park, the purpose being to organize people who traveled the roads for fun and recreation. Two meetings were held each year—a summer one in Michigan and the other a winter gathering in Florida. Members were distinguished by the tin cans soldered onto their radiator caps. Traverse City was the primary host town in Michigan, while various towns competed to host the Florida gatherings. Also, tin can tourist camps popped up in various locations, such as Gainesville and Tallahassee, promoted by savvy politicians and businessmen who realized the potential economic impacts. The camps often featured a bathhouse, community center, laundry, store, and sometimes rental cabins. Besides purchasing food at local stores and produce stands, tin can tourists in remote areas often supplemented their protein with freshly caught fish.

At later statewide TCT gatherings, camping trailer dealers would set up displays in hopes of enticing tin canners to purchase the latest models. There were huge barbecues and group games such as shuffleboard and horseshoes. The WPA's 1939 guide to Florida concluded, "A spirit of comradeship, often lacking in the more expensive tourist centers of the State, is evident as the trailer folk gather in their camps and exchange tales of Nationwide wanderings."

The main thoroughfare at the Fort De Soto Camp was labeled "Easy Street," so tin can campers could write friends and family at home and honestly say they were "living on Easy Street." The Fort De Soto Camp underscored the fact that the St. Petersburg area was widely considered Florida's tourist capital in the early 1900s, grossing more than $50 million from tourism by 1940. Promoters billed it

An early St. Petersburg promotional booklet.

Published by E. C. Kropp Co. of Milwaukee; no date

as "The Sunshine City," and the local newspaper publisher promised a free afternoon paper if the sun failed to show by 3 p.m. For a twenty-six-year period, from 1913 to 1939, the publisher gave away fewer than five editions a year to make good on that promise.

Besides the weather, the St. Petersburg area boasted beaches, boating and fishing opportunities, free outdoor concerts, a flowing artesian well that promoters labeled "the fountain of youth," New York Yankees spring training games that originally included home-run hitter Babe Ruth, and an "air-cooled" Florida Theater that opened in 1926. The city also put in place more than five thousand "green benches" where visitors—mostly silver-haired snowbirds—could sit and relax down-

A circa 1915 postcard of St. Petersburg's "Fountain of Youth," styled after the Ponce de León legend. Several other Florida communities claim to have the original fountain of youth as well, prompting one observer to proclaim that the "fountain of kitsch" springs eternal.

town, a move that "converted the city into a park," according to the WPA. This guidebook added, "These slatted divans serve as mediums of introduction, with the weather the opening and principal topic. Operations, symptoms, and remedies run a close second. The benches are the open-air offices of the promoter, the hunting grounds of the real-estate 'bird dog,' a haven for the lonely, and a matrimonial bureau for many. They have figured in fiction, swindles, and divorce courts." Another popular gathering spot was the "million-dollar pier" along the Gulf of Mexico.

While tin canners could enjoy area attractions from their base camp—although at times local officials would close the camp since it did little to promote the city as a desirable location for more well-heeled tourists—wealthier visitors could stay in one of ten luxury hotels that included the Don CeSar ("The Don"), Vinoy, and Rolyat.

By the late 1920s, Americans had registered twenty-three million cars, and they were eager to explore the bounds of their new freedom. Eventually, St. Petersburg's tourism prominence diminished as more of the Sunshine State became accessible. Innumerable tourist attractions were developed, and existing ones were expanded. Silver Springs, for example, became a roadside attraction with broad appeal after two Ocala business-

Postcard showing a midwinter band concert in St. Petersburg, circa 1915.

men, W. C. Ray and W. M. Davidson, purchased the springs area in 1924.

Ray and Davidson built gasoline-powered glass-bottom boats that could fit larger numbers of people. A 1935 publication, *Shrine of the Water Gods*, describes the experience: "Once afloat, peering down at the bottom, one gets the effect of riding high aloft on some magic carpet, sliding along smoothly and silently over a vast valley. Far below, as though viewed through thin air—so transparent is the water—many varieties of fish swim lazily, or dart up to gaze momentarily with round, unblinking eyes at the strange creatures who have come to stare down at them."

But bigger and better glass-bottom boat rides were only the beginning. A concessionaire contract was signed with "Colonel Tooey" to start jungle

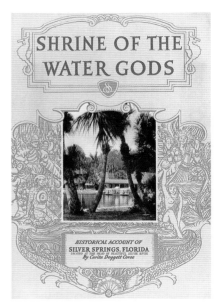

The Shrine of the Water Gods *booklet described the history of Silver Springs and was reprinted several times by Brown & Bigelow of St. Paul, Minnesota (no date).*

SS-21   ROSS ALLEN AND TRAINED SEAL UNDERWATER AT FLORIDA'S FAMED SILVER SPRINGS

1949 postcard showing Ross Allen and a seal.

cruise boat rides, and they became instantly popular. Tooey released rhesus macaque monkeys on a river island as an exotic bonus for visitors on the boat tours, but he didn't realize that rhesus monkeys are good swimmers. The primates escaped and began reproducing in the region. They've been a curious anomaly—and periodic management nuisance—ever since.

Florida had already gained a reputation as a reptile paradise, so Ray and Davidson became enamored with a nearly broke young herpetologist named Ross Allen who approached them in 1929. Allen's Ross Allen Reptile Institute soon became synonymous with Silver Springs as he held daily demonstrations and lectures with snakes, alligators, crocodiles, and turtles. A fan favorite was the "milking" of rattlesnakes for their venom, to be used to make antivenin and as a substitute for morphine for certain medical conditions. At one point, it is said that Allen's collection numbered around two thousand snakes, alligators, crocodiles, and turtles. Allen purchased native snakes, paying the most for large diamondback and canebrake rattlesnakes. In turn, he sold live snakes and other reptiles to tourists, clinics, and zoos. He even began flying to South America to collect anacondas and other animals for his institute and to sell to interested buyers. An early postcard showed him underwater with a trained seal, so he was not averse to featuring mammals either.

Ross Allen milking a snake, from a vintage Silver Springs brochure.

The Reptile Institute's 1939 price guide reveals the diversity and depth of Allen's collection. You could buy a diamondback rattlesnake for $1–$3 (depending on size), a coral snake for $3–$5, a box of eight assorted snakes more than four feet long for $10, and ten small but colorful snakes for $2.50. A kid could take home a cute baby alligator for a quarter and a two-foot baby crocodile for seventy-five cents. Larger gators and crocodiles were available for purchase, of course, with hefty sums charged for ten- and twelve-footers, but a black widow spider was only half a buck. Obviously, the simpler times also meant fewer regulations and lawsuits. Liability insurance was either inexpensive or nonexistent.

As the years progressed, Ross Allen became a larger-than-life Florida icon, enhanced by his frequent appearances in newsreels and on radio and television, known also for his daredevil shows with dangerous reptiles. Marjorie Kinnan Rawlings wrote in *Cross Creek* about how she accompanied Allen on a rattlesnake-catching expedition in the Everglades. "I shall always feel an interest in snakes, after my exposure to Ross' wisdom and knowledge," she concluded, "but it will never extend to making one welcome in the house."

In 1962, at age fifty-four, Allen led a highly publicized Florida "Survival Safari" on foot from the Atlantic coast to the Gulf of Mexico with a handpicked group of Boy Scouts. For thirteen days in June, the group trudged 153 miles, swimming across rivers and creeks and obtaining all of their food and shelter from the environment. Group meals included a variety of wild fruits and seeds along with roasted armadillos, frogs, pond snails, mussels, squirrels, grasshoppers, gopher tortoises, freshwater eels, skunks, rabbits, freshwater clams, fish, crabs, turtles, wild pigs, and a variety of snakes, including rattlesnakes, coral snakes, and water moccasins. The trip only enhanced Allen's reputation.

Allen developed a Seminole Indian camp on the south end of Silver Springs, recruiting Seminoles from the Everglades. Eventually, a pioneer camp and a replica of Fort King, an important base for the U.S. Army during the Second Seminole War, were erected. These became stops on the jungle boat tours. More animal exhibits, rides, and

UNDERWATER ARCHERY, SILVER SPRINGS, FLORIDA F-128

The crystal-clear waters of Silver Springs inspired novel promotional activities, including underwater archery.

a water park would follow. Since Silver Springs was once considered a remote destination, the idea was to keep visitors there longer and draw as much money from them as possible. Other tourist attractions near Silver Springs helped to attract and keep tourists for extended stays, the most notable being Six Gun Territory, an "Old West" town complete with dancing saloon girls and shootouts in the street.

For African Americans during the Jim Crow era, there was Paradise Park just downriver from the main springs, which offered similar boat rides and snake shows. "The Black culture before Civil Rights was a town within a town, a culture within a culture," said Reginald Lewis on the public television show *Florida Crossroads* in 2014. His grandfather managed Paradise

Park. "We might not have had the best, but we did good with everything we had. . . . It was a family-type place. My grandfather always believed in the people."

For African American tourists, travel was riskier and often less spontaneous since it was frequently to specific "colored" attractions such as American Beach on Amelia Island, Manhattan Beach near Mayport, Lincoln Park in Jacksonville, Butler Beach near St. Augustine, and several jazz clubs and casinos in large cities. Paradise Park was one of the few that flourished alongside a known attraction in Florida's interior. Many attractions, such as Wakulla Springs and Weeki Wachee, employed African Americans as boat drivers and other workers before people of color were allowed to

Old riverboats can still be seen docked at Silver Springs.

Doug Alderson

enter as visitors. And since Jim Crow laws affected state parks as well, separate state parks were sometimes developed for African Americans, such as Magnolia Lake State Park near Keystone Heights. Or there were segregated beaches, restrooms, and picnic areas within the same state park, such as at Little Talbot near Jacksonville and Florida Caverns near Marianna. However, national parks and other federal recreational facilities largely operated on a nondiscriminatory basis.

Hollywood discovered Silver Springs beginning in the 1930s, and scenes for at least twenty movies and various television shows were filmed there, including *Rebel without a Cause, The Yearling, Distant Drums*, the James Bond movie *Moonraker, Creature from the Black Lagoon* (along with Wakulla Springs), episodes of *Sea Hunt*, and six Tarzan flicks featuring Olympic swimming gold medalist Johnny Weissmuller.

Guess who filled in for Weissmuller during risky Tarzan scenes? Ross Allen, of course.

Barbara Lindner Wood was an Ocala high school student when she met Weissmuller at Silver Springs. "While working on location in Florida Weissmuller swam the Silver River almost every day to keep in shape and find relief from the drudgery of all that swinging in trees," she wrote in her memoir. "One day I was thrilled when he said, 'Do you want to swim with me?' Others had gone down the river with him, but most had been unable to complete the swim back against the swift current, having to steer themselves to the slippery bank and walk back to the Springs. I was determined to swim both ways and I did. From then on, if I was there, he would call, 'Come on with me.' Going down, we would swim side by side. On the return I lagged behind, but I always finished." Weissmuller provided Wood with swimming tips, and she went on to win several high school swim meets.

By the 1940s, Silver Springs was considered Florida's number one tourist destination, as evidenced by this description in a statewide tourist brochure from the era: "Florida's largest and most heavily patronized scenic attraction, Silver Springs is to the South what Niagara is to the East and Grand Canyon is to the West—internationally renowned." Silver Springs postcards were printed in Spanish, Portuguese, German, and English. Brochures were printed in quantities of seven million at a shot, and Silver Springs billboards stretched all the way to Maine. Observers commented that nearly every tourist car that left Florida seemed to display a Silver Springs bumper sticker.

Silver Springs became the anchor for a groundswell of Florida tourism. An understandable lull occurred during World War II, but the industry roared back to life in 1946 as both auto and air travel expanded. The postwar years leading up to the opening of Disney's theme parks in the Orlando area are often looked upon as Florida's golden age of tourism, and it is an era that still has a pulse, as we shall see in later chapters.

Present-day ruins of the replica of Fort King created at Silver Springs during its heyday.

Doug Alderson

THREE

History and Nature for All

<><><><><><><><><><><>

"Long, dreamy streets, bright, luxuriant flowers, heavy odors, languor-compelling air, blue sky, white sands, clumsy palm trees, a general attitude of complete relaxation on the broad bosom of Good Mother Nature; this is the atmosphere of 'Old St. Augustine.'"

John Martin Hammond,
Winter Journeys in the South (1916)

Most of Florida's early tourist attractions focused on what was natural, abundant, and unusual in Florida—springs, rivers, swamps, palm trees, alligators, birds, and fish. Eventually, some key Florida leaders began to realize that the wanton draining and clear-cutting of the Florida environment and destruction of its fish and wildlife populations that marked the late 1800s and early 1900s was unsustainable. Tourists or residents weren't going to continue to enjoy what was unique and natural about the Sunshine State if nothing was left of the giant cypresses or vast flocks of wading birds or if they could catch nary a fish.

In 1903, President Theodore Roosevelt established the first national wildlife refuge at Pelican Island in Florida's Indian River Lagoon. Brown pelicans, along with most other wading birds, were being slaughtered for their plumes, and Roosevelt sought to protect that last remaining rookery on the East Coast. A dedicated volunteer and later a ranger, German immigrant Paul Kroegel, made it his life's work to protect the island's pelicans from poachers.

More Florida refuges, along with national parks and monuments, followed. The Castillo de San Marcos in St. Augustine, a 1700s-era Spanish fort, became a national monument in 1924. Wrote C. R. Vinten, southeastern national monument coordinator, in 1947:

> *Our experience with operations at the Castillo has proven the value of working out a program around*

A DAY'S CATCH IN FLORIDA.

Published by Leighton & Valentine Company, New York City

Postcard showing early Florida fishermen and catch, postmarked 1911, before conservation laws were enacted.

the elements of greatest public interest. It has not been done without considerable pressure from those who have conflicting ideas. We could plant flower gardens on the City Gates, dress our personnel as Spanish Conquistadors, "restore" the Castillo as it was in 1700, cut up the Fort Green into softball diamonds and tennis courts, fly Spanish flags around the ramparts, exhibit wax figures of prisoners in the dungeons and priests in the chapel, change the museum front from a simple device for illustrating the story to a collection of ancient artifacts, and follow many other ideas that may have considerable merit in themselves; but it seems wiser to give the visitor a simple picture of why the Castillo was built, how it protected Spanish Florida, and what part it played in the history of America.

Vinten described a national monument as an area set aside to "preserve and protect the scene at one of the great moments in our national history—to stop the clock and hold the scene of the moment in history that makes the area important."

St. Augustine was all about history. Not only did it feature the Castillo de San Marcos, but it also claimed the oldest European-American house, oldest schoolhouse, oldest store, and several other historical buildings. In the 1880s, St. Augustine became a popular destination for wealthy tourists to winter at because the train line at the time didn't go any farther south.

French writer Paul Bourget described the city's luxury hotels in 1894:

"At this moment, although the end of the winter season is at hand, the traveler can scarcely find room in these palace-like buildings, one of which resembles the Alcazar, another the Alhambra, a third the Escurial, a fourth a vast house of the colonial period. And all is on a scale of extravagant luxury which all the travelers visibly enjoy. . . . After dinner a ball is organized, and they all dance."

In 1916, St. Augustine still had a bustling tourist trade, as evidenced by the account by John Martin Hammond in *Winter Journeys in the South*:

> The charm of St. Augustine is
> unmistakable and omnipresent.
> Once one has sensed, once one
> has heard it, amidst the confusion
> and over all the hubbub of the
> vulgar every-day life of the place,
> it calls like the refrain of some

> good music in the mind while one
> is walking down a noisy street. For
> my part I believe that I would like
> St. Augustine better during the
> summer when the winter visitors
> are not on hand, for during the
> "season" it is almost impossible to
> see the place for the people. It is
> difficult then to enter in spirit into
> the life of the city and dream, as
> the old city assuredly does, of the
> days when the banner of proud
> Spain waved over the ramparts
> of old Fort Marion, of the days
> when swash-buckling buccaneers
> in the adjacent waters were a
> reality, though maybe not so
> picturesque a reality as distance
> has painted them, when old
> Spain was a young Spain, and all
> the world held simple ideas and
> unsophisticated guests.

Courtyard of the former Alcazar Hotel.

Doug Alderson

Ornate domed ceiling inside the former Ponce de León Hotel in St. Augustine, now Flagler College.

Doug Alderson

While history was being preserved for Florida visitors and residents, the largest national park in Florida was established in 1947: the Everglades. For decades state officials and private developers had sought to drain the vast wetlands to create farmland and cities, viewing it as wasteland, but naturalists, visitors, and writers had differing opinions. In 1884, in *Camping and Cruising in Florida*, James A. Henshall wrote:

> *But it is not for the invalid alone that this region has attractions, but for the tourist, the sportsman, the lover of adventure, and the settler as well. The country from Miami to Cape Sable is known as the Indian Hunting Grounds, and abounds in game of all kinds common to the climate, and where it roams almost undisturbed. . . .*
>
> *The singular and wonderful region known as the Everglades is not, as is popularly supposed, an impenetrable swamp, exhaling an atmosphere of poisonous gases and deadly miasma, but a charming, shallow lake of great extent, with pure and limpid waters from a few inches to several feet in depth, in which grow curious water-grasses and beautiful aquatic plants; while thousands of small islands, from a few rods to a hundred acres in extent, rise from the clear waters, clothed with never-ending verdure and flowers.*

Marjory Stoneman Douglas was credited as being a major motivational force behind the creation of Everglades National Park. "There are no other Everglades in the world," Douglas began her classic *The Everglades: River of Grass*. "They are, they have always been one of the unique regions of the earth, remote, never wholly known. Nothing anywhere else is like them: their vast glittering openness, wider than the enormous visible round of the horizon, the racing free saltness and sweetness of their massive winds, under the dazzling blue heights of space."

Vintage postcard, postmarked 1909, of Sallie's Observation Tower in the Everglades.

The "Sallies" Observatory out on the Everglades, Everglade Trips, Miami, Fla.

Published by C. B. Pennock of Miami

At the 1947 Everglades National Park dedication, President Harry Truman was the headline attraction. "Here is land, tranquil in its quiet beauty, serving not as the source of water, but as the last receiver of it. To its natural abundance we owe the spectacular plant and animal life that distinguishes this place from all others in our country," he said.

Florida governor and park supporter Millard Caldwell saw the potential of establishing a national park in the country's largest remaining subtropical wilderness. The park would "prove to be of tremendous economic importance to the state and every effort should be made to expand its scope and enhance its value. It will be unique among the parks of the country and will attract visitors year round." Year-round visitation was hampered, however, by healthy crops of mosquitoes, a condition that persists today. It was likely no accident that the dedication occurred in December.

At the state level, the Florida Forest Service was established in 1928, the Florida Game and Freshwater Fish Commission (now the Florida Fish and Wildlife Conservation Commission) was created in 1935 to regulate hunting and fishing, and the Florida Park Service was created that same year. The state had already protected some state lands, such as the Olustee Battlefield site in 1899, followed by the Dade Battlefield, Natural Bridge Battlefield, Royal Palm Hammock, and Gamble Plantation. These lands and others were first protected by citizens' groups, indicating to state leaders the demand for access to natural and historical sites. "If paradise can't be preserved in its entirety," wrote former Florida Park Service director Ney

Landrum in *A Legacy of Green*, "maybe some of its choice parts could at least be preserved separately."

After the Florida Park Service was formally established by the Florida legislature in 1935, the first seven state parks to be created were Myakka River and Highlands Hammock in South Florida, Hillsborough River in central Florida, Gold Head Branch and Fort Clinch in Northeast Florida, and Torreya and Florida Caverns in the Florida Panhandle. The timing was impeccable. Since the nation was in the throes of the Great Depression, jobless men were put to work in the Civilian Conservation Corps (CCC). Developing amenities and attractions at state parks constituted perfect CCC projects.

Stone bridge in Torreya State Park built by the Civilian Conservation Corps.

Doug Alderson

The Gregory Mansion, reconstructed in Torreya State Park by the Civilian Conservation Corps.

Along the Apalachicola River, the CCC dismantled an abandoned plantation house and floated it piece by piece to a high bluff in Torreya State Park. It was painstakingly rebuilt and restored, and the Gregory House remains a draw for visitors. The CCC also built a Roman-style stone bridge in the park that is now a featured stop along a hiking trail.

At Florida Caverns, near Marianna in the Panhandle, CCC workers used chisels, shovels, and pickaxes to enlarge several passageways in the main tour cavern. The marks of their careful work can still be seen on some of the cave walls. North of Jacksonville at Fort Clinch, the CCC removed huge amounts of sand from the fort and turned the storehouse into the first state park museum and library. In total, the CCC constructed ninety-nine

buildings at the first seven state parks and nearly all the other amenities. Native materials such as cypress and limestone were extensively used. A CCC forestry camp was established at Oleno, which eventually became a state park. Suwannee River and Tomoka had been added as state parks by 1938.

Highlands Hammock State Park shows up on many of the old tourist brochures. It was protected by local citizens in 1931, and the CCC built facilities and began working on a botanical garden in 1934. It became a state park a year later. The state CCC Museum is located within the park.

Nearly from the beginning, the Florida Park Service generated revenue from its admissions and fees. In 1939, admission to most parks ranged from twenty-five cents per car at Hillsborough River State Park to thirty-five

Cave scene at Florida Caverns State Park.

Doug Alderson

Doug Alderson

Wall of a cave in Florida Caverns State Park showing chisel marks made by CCC workers.

Old Dixie Highway
Tomoka State Park
Daytona Beach, Florida

Early postcard showing the Old Dixie Highway through Tomoka State Park.

cents per car and driver at Highlands Hammock and fifteen cents for each additional passenger. At the parks that featured camping, fees were generally twenty-five cents per night or $1 a week, and cabin rentals ranged from $1.50 to $3 a night.

According to park service director Lewis G. Scoggin in 1947, the far-reaching mission of the Florida Park Service should be to "acquire remaining unspoiled typical portions of Florida's original domain before they are forever spoiled or lost; and in such acreage and in such locations as will be accessible to all the people of Florida . . . [to c]onserve these natural values for all time."

Scoggin further outlined a visionary philosophy that would help to shape the park service for decades by stating that an adequate state park system should provide a state park "within fifty miles of every citizen of Florida."

When Florida's open-range era officially ended around 1949, this inadvertently closed Florida's vast private landscapes and waterfronts to untold numbers of tent campers, making them more reliant on public lands. Thus, increased emphasis was placed on adding camping opportunities at Florida state parks.

The state park system expanded despite receiving the lowest stipend of any state agency for several years. "We are the newest addition to the family who was told he must survive on one meal a week while his sisters and brothers ate three sumptuously daily and lived on in comparative luxury," parks board chairman John D. Pennekamp lamented in a 1950 speech. Volunteers were then, as they

Postcard photo taken around 1910; no publisher listed

Many unique Florida landscapes such as Paynes Prairie near Gainesville became Florida state parks.

are now, key to the system's survival. Pennekamp continued:

> Those who are not coming here are for the most part unaware that the natural charm and appeal of this state with which they became acquainted in the history books and geographies of their school days still remain and are available to them.
>
> Our State Park System embraces the tangibles which appeal to them. But by reason of the crippling finances imposed upon us we have been able to operate at only about 10 percent of our potential.

By 1953, visitation at Florida state parks topped one million. Almost one-third of the overall attendance was derived from one park—Hugh Taylor Birch near Fort Lauderdale. This was the first coastal beach park in Southeast Florida, and its popularity underscored the allure of Florida's white-sand beaches.

By 1963, fifty-five state park units had been established; by 2019, the number stood at 175 state parks and state trails, with total annual visitation of more than twenty-nine million, topping Disney World's annual visitation by several million. The expansion of the park system was partly due to ambitious land-buying programs, helping to meet the growing demand for authentic ecotourism adventures, be they guided hikes through wilderness swamps such as the Fakahatchee Strand or kayak and canoe trips down canopied rivers or along wild coastlines.

Early Florida state park brochure, circa early 1960s.

Jim Stevenson, one of the Florida Park Service's high-profile ambassadors in the latter half of the twentieth century, described the balancing act between park development and resource protection in his 2013 memoir: "There was a constant tension between those who wanted more recreational use and the naturalists who wanted more protection of natural values. This tug-of-war actually resulted in better development, use, and management of the parks. Examples include tubing management at Ichetucknee Springs, manatee protection at Blue Spring, mosquito control in coastal parks, and Australian pine removal at John Pennekamp."

In the 1990s and 2000s, a growing demand for bicycle trails began to emerge among residents and tourists alike. A network of paved, off-road trails started to be built across the state ranging from the Blackwater Heritage State Trail near Pensacola to the Florida Keys Overseas Heritage Trail to the 250-mile Florida Coast-to-Coast Trail from St. Petersburg to Titusville. The longer the trail, the more it became a destination in itself, and this concept was mirrored by development of the 1,300-mile Florida National Scenic Trail, primarily for hikers, and the 1,515-mile Florida Circumnavigational Saltwater Paddling Trail, which stretched around Florida's entire coast. Former railroad and steamboat destination towns such as Palatka, Winter Garden, Titusville, and Dunedin began

emerging as prominent recreational trail towns in the twenty-first century, and their local economies picked up as a result.

At state parks, preserves, and refuges, one could see colorful animals ranging from alligators to manatees, a real draw for Florida tourists. According to a 2016–2017 survey, 59 percent of Florida visitors participated in wildlife-viewing activities, making it the second-most popular leisure activity behind beach-going. This meant a huge economic boost to Florida to the tune of $5.8 billion a year, according to the Outdoor Industry Association.

"Heritage tourism" that focuses on Florida's history and culture is a growing business as well, generating billons in annual revenues. About half of Florida's four-hundred-plus museums are historical in nature, and fifteen hundred sites are listed on the

Reenactments of battles in the Second Seminole War and Civil War are popular in the state, such as this Civil War battle reenactment at Natural Bridge near Tallahassee.

Doug Alderson

National Register of Historic Places. Annual reenactments of Seminole War and Civil War battles are held in key locations such as the Olustee Battlefield near Lake City, the Dade Battlefield State Park near Bushnell, and the Big Cypress Shootout on the Big Cypress Seminole Reservation. Many other sites have ongoing living-history interpreters, whether it is the Spanish mission site of San Luis or the Tallahassee Museum in Tallahassee, Marjorie Kinnan Rawlings's homestead at Cross Creek, or Cracker Country in Tampa. These places give visitors a look and feel of historical time periods and traditional lifestyles.

After a few days at Disney World and other fantasy theme parks, many tourists yearn for a "real Florida" experience, and they are finding ample opportunities in the state's natural areas and historical sites. "Florida is for amazement, wonder and delight, and refreshment of the soul," wrote author Ernest Lyons in 1969. "It may take a little more time to hunt out and enjoy the real Florida, but you will be well repaid."

FOUR

Other Lands and Worlds

◇◇◇◇◇◇◇◇◇◇◇◇◇◇◇◇◇◇

"Neither tourism nor nature is destiny. In the end, tourism relies upon manufactured images, carefully crafted and packaged."

Gary Mormino, *Land of Sunshine, State of Dreams (2005)*

While public agencies and other entities were protecting and featuring "the real Florida," private groups and wealthy individuals were making full use of Florida's subtropical climate to create elaborate gardens—often adding other amenities—and turning them into attractions. Initially, perhaps it was an attempt at escapism—escape from the ravages of the Great Depression, escape to a far-off land one could never afford to visit, or escape to a fantasy land that only existed on the silver screen and in the human imagination. Regardless, Florida was a rich garden—a southern Eden—upon which dreams could be planted, and many are still growing.

The Singing Tower (later referred to as Bok Tower) utilized a natural landmark—"Iron Mountain," one of peninsular Florida's highest points at 298 feet above sea level. It was part of

Edward Bok's "Mountain Lake Sanctuary" near Lake Wales, dedicated by President Calvin Coolidge in 1929. The ornate 205-foot tower was built of Florida coquina stone and Georgia pink marble and contained a sixty-bell carillon. A large pool in front of the tower bordered by flowering shrubs provided a serene reflection. Mr. Bok donated his sanctuary to the public "simply to create symbols of pure beauty, so as to spread the influence and power of beauty." And if you've ever purchased a collection of vintage postcards, Bok appears to have succeeded. Bok Tower, reflecting in the pool, is likely the most common postcard image you'll find. According to author Tracy Revels, the Bok Tower and accompanying gardens "was the first major attraction created to be a novelty. Bearing no direct relationship to the climate, history, native peoples, or natural wonders of Florida,

Vintage Bok Tower orange crate label.

Doug Alderson

it was built purely to be a landmark and lure visitors. Future attractions would follow its example, if not its aesthetic qualities."

The description may be a bit harsh since the garden bird list totals 126 species, most of them native, making it a designated site on the Great Florida Birding and Wildlife Trail, and Bok Tower Gardens is a leader in the conservation of rare native plants. Bok also shied away from overt commercialization and allowed for free entry for several years. (We'll learn more about this subject in a later chapter.)

Seven years after Bok's garden was opened, a Winter Haven attraction came on the scene and would become Florida's most famous "garden." Founder Dick Pope and his wife, Julie, initially purchased sixteen acres along the shores of Lake Eloise. After

draining wetlands, carving canals, and planting thousands of flowering plants, trees, and shrubs, the colorful Pope vowed to "make a real Venice out of the place." Not only did Cypress Gardens become a "botanical wonderland," but it also became famous for hoop-skirted beauties, quiet electric boat rides along the cypress-ringed lake, and daredevil water shows. And the advertising blitz Pope launched created an amalgamation of nature and Madison Avenue. During its peak, hundreds of publicity photos were sent out daily. Eight photographers were employed, partly to help visitors load their film, and the attraction was the top seller of Kodak film in the United States. At one point, Pope himself had 1.5 million negatives in his vault.

The southern belles that became associated with the attraction came about by accident. A 1940 freeze left dead vines and other unsightly foliage near the front gate, so Dick Pope asked the young women working at the attraction to put on their best skirts and to stand in front and wave at people. It worked. Instead of turning away at the sight of the freeze damage, visitors fixated on the pretty young women and had no hesitation about entering the park. A tradition was born, and other attractions started making full use of lovely young women.

In 1943, the renowned water-skiing shows were added by accident as well. A water-skiing photo from the lake was published in a local paper, and some servicemen came to the gardens to see more. The problem was that the water skiers were not affiliated with the attraction. At the time, Dick Pope was overseas as part of the war effort, so his wife, Julie, was at the helm. She asked her children and their friends to ski and perform whatever daredevil stunts they could muster. The kids were popular enough to draw more servicemen the next day, and a landmark attraction was born. For the next few decades, when people thought of Cypress Gardens, elaborate water-skiing shows were usually the first images that came forward.

Soon after Dick Pope returned home, he took full advantage of Florida's postwar tourism boom. He began cranking out publicity photos to the tune of five hundred a day. He also noticed that most of the backdrops for Hollywood movies were the hills of Burbank. For some diversity, Pope offered to allow film companies to use Cypress Gardens as a backdrop for free as long as they mentioned the attraction. Subsequently, several movies were filmed there, among them two with renowned swimmer Esther Williams. A Florida-shaped pool was built for her use, which became another trademark attraction. Elvis Presley, Betty Grable, and King Hussein of Jordan were among the celebrity guests. Even Johnny Carson filmed the first color episode of *The Tonight Show* at Cypress Gardens, and the most popular television daytime talk show of the late 1960s, *The Mike Douglas Show*, filmed an entire week's worth of shows at the attraction on two different occasions. Guest stars included Muhammad Ali and Duke Ellington. The Popes and their attraction were riding high, and it was apparent why Dick Pope had earned the nicknames "the father of Florida tourism," "Mr. Water Skiing," "Mr. Florida," and "the man who invented Florida."

Naturally, Pope's opinion was sought when Walt Disney's plans for a "magic kingdom" became known in 1965. "Anyone who is going to spend $100 million near me is good, and a good thing," he said. His words seemed prophetic. Soon after Walt Disney's Magic Kingdom opened in 1971, attendance at Cypress Gardens rose steadily, peaking in 1976 when a record 1.7 million visitors paid admission. The next year, attendance dropped by almost half a million. It rose and fell for a couple more years as the attraction launched a major expansion, but by 1984 a steady decline had begun, and Dick Pope died in 1988.

In 2004, the struggling attraction was being considered for a state park. A debate, centering on whether all or part of the attraction would be purchased using state Florida Forever money, raged for several months. Hoop-skirted Cypress Gardens beauties, world-renowned water skiers, Dick Pope Jr., local officials, and supporters eager to restore lost jobs paraded to Tallahassee to influence decision-makers. "This is old Florida," Burma Davis Posey, president of Friends of Cypress Gardens, told a state land-buying panel. "This is what our state is about and once it's gone, it's gone forever."

Governor Jeb Bush, a recipient of thousands of e-mails, petitions, and calls from Cypress Gardens proponents, favored state purchase of at least part of the site, but some conservationists were more cautious. Florida Forever was originally created in 1998 to conserve environmentally sensitive, undeveloped land and water resources. Cultural and historical landmarks were added a year later. "It's for conservation, not amusement rides," said Mary Ann Ryan of the Sierra Club. "The original botanical gardens and open space along the lake has value to us, but if it's expanded beyond that, we say absolutely not." Polk County ended up purchasing thirty acres of the historical gardens, and the state of Florida bought development rights for 150 acres, but no state park was established.

Kent Buescher, owner of Wild Adventures near Valdosta, Georgia, purchased the attraction that year and came through with an ambitious plan to add rides as a way to boost attendance. Cypress Gardens had new life, and almost everyone seemed happy, but then four hurricanes struck in 2004 in quick succession—Charley, Frances, Ivan, and Jeanne. Three of the storms crossed Polk County, home of Cypress Gardens, and the revitalized park sustained major damage, especially from Charley. After a long delay and an expensive recovery effort, Buescher's Florida venture opened briefly to great fanfare. Besides the traditional Cypress Gardens venues of gravity-defying water-skiing shows, beautiful gardens, guided boat rides, and southern beauties, thrilling roller coasters such as the "Triple Hurricane" had been added to bring in a younger crowd. "Kent Buescher and his group have woven a beautiful tapestry of old and new so that Cypress Gardens now has something for every taste," concluded Bill Vanderford of the *Forsyth County News*.

But Buescher had stretched his credit line thin with the repairs and additions, and insurance companies paid only a portion of his $25 million in claims attributed to the hurricanes. He filed for bankruptcy in 2006 and soon retreated to his successful Wild Adventures near Valdosta. Former state senator Rick Dantzler of Winter Haven, who had married into the Pope family, called it a "perfect storm of misfortune." A new owner took over the site in 2007, but that buyer, too, went belly up and sold out in 2010 to Merlin Entertainment Group, creators of LEGOLAND (see chapter 9).

Tampa lawyer J. William Dupree got into the gardens business by accident—literally. He had purchased a nine-hundred-acre estate near Land O' Lakes north of Tampa and then got into a car wreck. Gardening helped him to recover, and friends encouraged him to open his work to the public, like many of Florida's garden attractions, which he did in 1940. Dupree added a restaurant, piped-in classical music, and boat rides on his private lake.

For a "South Sea Island Paradise in Florida," visitors flocked to Tiki Gardens between Clearwater and St. Petersburg, complete with thatched huts and tribal statues. In the Tallahassee area there was the "Garden of Mystery," according to one website, but details about its original whereabouts remain shrouded in mystery.

Most of the otherworldly attractions in the Panhandle centered around Panama City Beach's Miracle Strip. Jungle Land opened in 1966 with a bang, featuring a smoking and flame-spitting volcano. Bathing beauties wore outfits that bore some resemblance to the classic Flintstones outfits of Wilma and Betty. Jungle Land lasted until the late 1970s, whereupon the volcano became a centerpiece for Alvin's Magic Mountain Mall.

Melody May was one of the primary models for bathing-beauty photos along the Miracle Strip in the 1960s and 1970s, including those at Jungle Land. May had just graduated from high school when auditions were held in 1965 at the Holiday Lodge along Panama City Beach. "They said we want to use you for two reasons—your smile and your legs," May said in 2014. "That was the start of it." The most famous photo of the era featured May's backside in a swimsuit with the Panama City Beach observation tower in the background. "Come see the other side," said the advertisement.

At one point, she posed with a blind fourteen-foot alligator. "They poked it and they said to look scared," she said. "I was." In one photo, she pretended to mail baby alligators. Photos of May appeared on postcards and in brochures, newspapers, and magazines throughout the county, even in *Stars and Stripes*, but she was paid very little. "I did it mostly for fun," she said. "People on the beach would want to take my photo when they saw me."

May later became an artist, mother, and grandmother, and she lamented many of the changes along the beach. "They should never have allowed the condos to be built on the beautiful sand dune areas," she said. "There's hardly any sand dunes or sea oats left, and a lot of the sand is gone. It was a fun family place then, and you could sleep on the beach and have bonfires." May passed away in early 2015 at age sixty-seven.

While the Miracle Strip, Fort Myers, Daytona Beach, Fort Lauderdale, and Miami Beach became famous draws for the beach crowd during Florida's golden age of tourism, exotic animals

Early Parrot Jungle brochure, front and back.

such as parrots and monkeys showed up in many of the garden attractions in the 1930s and 1940s. But these did not completely satiate tourist demands—or, rather, the ambitions of entrepreneurs. By the 1950s, Florida attractions were evoking the Serengeti of Africa, giving visitors more than just a taste of wild Florida and offering a land of roaming animal herds and man-eating predators that few would ever get to see in real life. "Jungle" would become a common theme for Florida attractions, connoting mysterious South Sea islands or the deep wilds of Africa.

Boca Raton was the site of Africa USA in 1954, featuring African animals, geysers, and waterfalls.

Busch Gardens, an Anheuser-Busch project, opened in 1959 in Tampa. It also featured imported African animals along with hundreds of exotic birds and the famous Clydesdale horses. A "monorail safari" was added

No source listed

and, after Disney opened, thrill rides. I think my dad enjoyed the free beer samples the most, a feature that only annual pass holders can enjoy today.

Jungle Larry's Safari opened in Naples in 1964 and was also advertised as a type of cageless zoo. The attraction became part of Caribbean Gardens in 1969, and after Larry's death in 1984, Larry's wife and children carried on the attraction.

Johnny Weissmuller, the early Tarzan actor, seemed a natural fit in Florida's jungle theme since he filmed several movies in the Sunshine State. After retiring from Hollywood, he returned to Florida to endorse Tropical Wonderland (formerly Florida Wonderland) near Titusville in 1971, bringing new life to the park. As one might expect, there were exotic African animals along with elements of several other Florida attractions—a snake farm, a trained dolphin act, amusement rides, and even an Old West–themed section

Above: Early Monkey Jungle brochure.

Right: Monkey Jungle postcard.

Published by Florida Natural Color, Inc. of Miami

DRIVE YOUR OWN CAR THROUGH

LION COUNTRY SAFARI

WEST PALM BEACH,
FLORIDA
AT
ROYAL PALM BEACH

Just off Florida Turnpike Exits 8 or 9

No source listed

Early Lion Country Safari brochure, circa late 1960s/early 1970s.

embargo was also in full swing, affecting tourism throughout the state. "We closed because the gas shortage limited tourist travel to the South," said park owner Ben Whitehouse. During the park's last gasp, neighbors complained of monkeys running wild, scavenging in their garbage, and a Russian bear escaped from the park and was struck by a car.

History was not immune to the otherworldly flair in Florida. With the popularity of westerns on television from the 1940s through the 1960s, several "Old West" towns were built as attractions. Since no one could experience the Old West except on the silver screen, the replica attractions served as fitting substitutes.

Along Panama City Beach's Miracle Strip, Lee Koplin started Tombstone Territory. It included a Spanish mission and statues, an adobe-style Indian village inside a mammoth man-made cave, a large totem pole, and—here's the strange juxtaposition again—a massive genie emerging from a lamp. The key was to grab the attention of tourists traveling U.S. 98, and it was largely successful.

Just down the road was Tombstone's chief rival, Petticoat Junction, also a western-themed attraction with an added bonus of amusement rides. I visited as a young teenager, but my attention was mostly on pretty girls (and there were plenty), so I didn't pay much attention to the train and other features. Petticoat Junction was named after a 1960s television sitcom that had nothing to do with the West, but the

that featured "actual hangings." Locals reported that Weissmuller would give his famous Tarzan yell in exchange for drinks at the Royal Oak Country Club.

Tropical Wonderland in Titusville began to sputter in 1973 and closed for good a year later when Weissmuller pulled his endorsement, citing mistreatment of animals. The Arab oil

Tombstone Territory in Panama City Beach competed with the neighboring Petticoat Junction attraction for Old West tourists.

show featured a steam-driven train and so did the attraction. Plus, the owner knew Edgar Buchanan, the show's star (Uncle Joe Carson) and occasional western actor. Buchanan helped the attraction receive permission to use the name. (Interestingly, Buchanan played Curly Bill Brocious in the 1942 western classic *Tombstone, the Town Too Tough to Die*.) For several years, the competing whistles of steam locomotives echoed across the Miracle Strip.

Perhaps the most famous Florida "Old West" town was Ocala's Six Gun Territory. It also had a train, shootouts in the streets, dancing saloon girls, and Indians on the warpath. We'll explore this attraction in more detail in the next chapter.

Along Florida's east coast, St. Augustine, a bona fide historical town with a long pedigree, added several nonhistoric features and some highly unusual historical twists to boost tourism. Near the top of the list was Zorayda Castle, described as a world-famous Moorish palace inspired by the Alhambra of Granada, Spain. First built as a winter residence in 1883, the castle included such featured attractions as a mummy's foot and a twenty-three-hundred-year-old sacred cat rug, found in the casket of a mummy in the Nile's Valley of the Kings and made from the hair of prehistoric four-foot-long cats.

A garish St. Augustine display was an exposed Native American mass burial, one that has since been covered due to protests from Native Americans. Similar attractions of this type around the country have, thankfully, also closed. St. Augustine likewise featured its oldest jail with graphic depictions of prison horrors.

When I was eleven years old, in 1968, my family visited St. Augustine and stayed at a typical-looking motor court with a pool. We accessed the downtown attraction by way of a little tourist tram pulled by a funny-looking truck. We visited the Castillo de San Marcos, one of the town's biggest draws, and it was crowded with visitors. Sometime after viewing the clammy room where Osceola and other Seminole leaders were imprisoned—

and from which many escaped—I got lost. After wandering aimlessly for a half hour or so, I assumed my parents and brothers had gotten back on the tourist tram, so I caught the next one.

The tram had other stops, and one was Ripley's Believe or Not!, established in St. Augustine in 1950 just after the opening of Potter's Wax Museum. I had always enjoyed the Ripley's features on the back of comic books, and so I got off to see the museum and to look for my family. I became caught up in viewing such illustrious displays as South American shrunken heads and the largest operational Ferris wheel built with an erector set. About two hours later, I got back on

Erected in 1959, this giant purple dinosaur at
Goofy Golf in Panama City Beach still stands tall.

Doug Alderson

the tram and arrived at the motel at sunset. Understandably, my parents were wracked with worry and gave me a good scolding, but I enjoyed my adventure through St. Augustine's mishmash of attractions. In later years, St. Augustine added popular ghost tours, and that would have been high on my to-do list.

Concrete dinosaurs became popular at Florida attractions in the 1950s, even though Florida was underwater during the epoch when dinosaurs roamed the earth. Dinosaurs decorated gas stations, miniature golf courses such as Goofy Golf in Panama City Beach,

gardens such as Tampa's Fairyland at Lowry Park, McKee Jungle Gardens in Vero Beach, and Bongoland, an amusement park in Port Orange along Florida's east coast. Founded in 1946, Bongoland also featured Spanish ruins, an Indian village, and a trained baboon named Bongo who greeted visitors and picked their pockets. Bongoland is now Sugar Mill Gardens, a botanical gardens and historical site operated by a nonprofit organization, but the concrete dinosaurs have remained. The Rain Forest north of Bushnell on U.S. 301 boasted animated dinosaurs lurking in the jungle along with a Sacred

Floridaland, in Osprey on the Gulf Coast, was a "theme park in search of a theme." It closed in 1971.   Published by Florida Natural Color Incorporated of Miami; no copyright

Art Garden that featured art painted in glass, gold, silver, brass, and mother-of-pearl. By 1970, only a solitary dinosaur watched over the closed buildings of the Rain Forest until the site became a country club.

The attraction that seemed to combine everything except for concrete dinosaurs was Floridaland on U.S. 41 between Sarasota and Venice. At Floridaland, you could find a porpoise show, a western ghost town, a cancan show, a petting zoo and "Goat Island," tropical gardens, a whiskey still, an Indian village, tram trains, and sea lions. What, no mermaids?

Floridaland splashed onto the scene in 1964 and was billed as "Everything You Came to Florida to See," although one critic said it "seemed to be a theme park in search of a theme." It died seven years after it opened, in 1971, being too much of a hodgepodge even by Florida standards. Perhaps the most notable achievement of Floridaland was having arranged the world's first "porpoise-to-porpoise" long-distance call. In May 1965, its star porpoise "Moby Dick" communicated in high-pitched tones for five minutes with Keiki at Sea Life Park in Hawaii, using a specially designed phone.

During Florida's golden age of tourism, the Sunshine State became a place to find not only wildness and natural beauty but also far-off lands, colorful time periods in history, and imaginary worlds—all for the price of admission. And, ironically, this growing perception of Florida as a land of fantasy and imagination opened the way for Walt Disney—the undisputed Dream King—to become firmly established in central Florida. Walt Disney World reshaped Florida's tourist landscape, and the mega–theme park era it ushered in wouldn't be kind to many of Florida's classic attractions, as we shall soon see.

FIVE
Gone Forever?

◇◇◇◇◇◇◇◇◇◇◇◇◇◇

The attraction I yearned to visit most as a boy but never did was Ocala's Six Gun Territory. What boy in the 1960s could resist shootouts in the streets, Indian war dances, and high-kicking saloon girls? Here's an excerpt from a 1960s-era brochure for the attraction: "It's blazing guns and thundering hoofs, red-satin ladies and tinkling nickelodeons, howling Indians and dusty burros, Conestoga wagons and stagecoaches—all at 6 Gun Territory, where you will become a part of an old Frontier Town."

Bonanza television stars Dan Blocker and Lorne Greene endorsed the attraction as one of the best Old West–style towns in existence, even though it sat next to Silver Springs in central Florida. Conceived by R. B. Coburn in 1963, the "town" was spread over 254 acres and included a locomotive trip and sky ride. Here's an endorsement from Dan Blocker: "I have appeared in rodeos, western towns through the United States, and I can certainly say that SIX GUN TERRITORY is one of the most authentic

Six Gun Territory brochure, circa mid-1960s.

and entertaining ghost towns of the old west I have ever visited."

Ghost town? Six Gun Territory was never a real town, nor was it in the Old West, but that's what attractions of this type were all about—stretching reality and creating a make-believe world. In this case, it was creating a world based upon decades of movie and television stereotypes all packed into one location. The main street consisted of forty real buildings—not movie-style facades—and they included a general store, jail, saloon, hotel, courthouse, Wells Fargo, and bank. These were authentic-looking backdrops for the gunfights. Also nearby were an Indian teepee village, a Mexican "border town," and carnival rides on the outskirts. Gift shops were numerous, and by the 1980s, these included Ann's Hat Shop, Six Gun Photo, Miss Kitty's Ice Cream Parlor, and the El Sombrero Café. The "Territory's" sister park was Ghost Town in the Sky located in Maggie Valley, North Carolina. Similar western-themed towns that were also designed by Six Gun creator Russell Pearson included Frontier City in Oklahoma City, Silver Dollar City near Branson, Missouri, and Frontier Land in Cherokee, North Carolina.

To create a time and geographic space separation, visitors would first arrive at a train station backdropped by a huge fake mountain that was 60 feet high and 250 feet long. The "mountain" was hollow, built from two-by-fours, chicken wire, and building mud. Understandably, no one was allowed to climb on it.

From the entrance station, visitors would be carried by a locomotive-pulled train almost two miles to the simulated western town, a ride abruptly interrupted by masked men who attempted

Postcard showing Six Gun Territory stagecoach and street scene.

a train robbery. For a time, an Italian imported sky ride assisted in hauling visitors back and forth, with the entrance station marked by a giant metal teepee on the roof.

Besides the gunfights, which often concluded with the comical Digger the Undertaker taking valuables from the bodies, entertainment included Indian-style dances, whip cracking, tomahawk- and knife-throwing demonstrations, and various shows in the air-conditioned Palace Saloon and Theatre and Red Dog Saloon. These indoor shows included cancan dances, musical revues, old-fashioned melodramas, country music acts, and comedy acts.

Tallahassee Democrat columnist Mark Hinson recalled a visit to Six Gun Territory when he was about five years old. The main attraction that day was Dan Blocker, the actor who played Hoss on *Bonanza*.

> *By the time our station wagon pulled into Six-Gun Territory, it was one of those belligerently hot and bright days in Florida when all you can do is squint and hope you don't bump into anything that is sharp or pointed. We native Floridians call that spring. We bought four black-and-white publicity photos of Blocker, who was posed in his full Hoss regalia, and waited in line for what felt like 10 hours.*
>
> *Being new to the glamorous world of celebrity, I thought we were going to get a private audience with Hoss. Meet the real*

Hoss, you know. Ask him if Hop Sing ever made cheese grits or how we could grow up and find a job like his, which, as far as I could tell, involved lifting heavy objects off of cowboys who were being crushed to death by wagon wheels.

> *Instead, we basted like pink shrimp in the sun along with hundreds of other broiling "Bonanza" fans. Blocker sat behind a large wooden table inside an empty house signing photo after photo. He was crankin' em out for the fans who filed through, cafeteria-style. My brothers and I were finally granted entry into the house of Hoss and were given a few seconds of face-time with the star. He was sweaty and a little glass-eyed as he gave us an uneven grin and scrawled his name unevenly on the photos. We were too star-struck to say anything. After a few seconds, we were whisked out the back door.*

Other western stars made appearances at Six Gun, including *Laramie* star John Smith, Frank McGrath of *Wagon Train*, and Michael Landon of *Bonanza*. Predominately nonwestern stars made appearances, too, such as Irene Ryan and Buddy Ebsen of the *Beverly Hillbillies*, Ron Howard of *The Andy Griffith Show* fame, and Luke Halpin of *Flipper*.

The last shootout at Six Gun Territory occurred in 1984, following the demise of western television shows. Two years after it became a true "ghost town," a shopping mall was built in

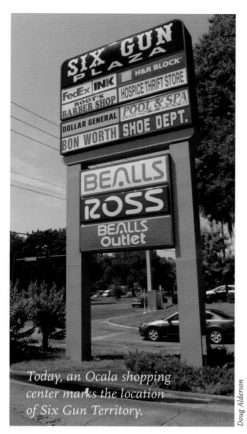

Today, an Ocala shopping center marks the location of Six Gun Territory.

Doug Alderson

Nostalgic films draw attention from other former visitors, who often write comments. "I was there about the second week of Sept in 1971," wrote John Saboruin. "I remember the date because we were 2 weeks early of the grand openings of Disney World. I remember riding the bumper cars and hitting the car my grandmother was driving . . . LOL. I also remember watching one of the gun fights and shortly after watching it I went around the corner in one of the stores and one of the cowboys was on a phone and when he saw me he drew on me. One of my greatest childhood memories was the day we went to Six Gun Territory."

Jeff Klinkenberg wrote, "The most successful tourist destinations today are generic 'anywhere USA' attractions that seldom have a relation to the region in which they're located." Six Gun Territory was always about a mythical place in a different region of the country; yet it still faded into the Florida sunset, an adopted son no more.

Interestingly, Six Gun Territory still survives in "real" life—in Michigan. It is run by White Hawk Ranch near Lexington and includes the usual Old West–style buildings along with a petting farm, pony rides, rope making, gold panning, and hay wagon and trolley rides. Not nearly as big in scope as the old Florida theme park and only open on summer weekends, it is a fun family place nonetheless.

Other peripheral attractions around Silver Springs also closed a few years after Disney World opened.

its place called "Six Gun Plaza," along with the Oak Hill Plantation subdivision on State Road 40 East. Most of the original Six Gun buildings were demolished and burned.

Former *Ocala Star-Banner* assistant editorial page editor Elaine Hamaker recalled Six Gun's final demise: "There was a kind of sadness about it all. Six Gun had been a landmark and there were a lot of fond memories here. It was all crumbling around me, bulldozers pushing buildings into the fire. It went out in a blaze of glory."

Six Gun Territory only lives on in memories now . . . and on YouTube.

These included Tommy Bartlett's Deer Ranch and the Prince of Peace Memorial. Even Ross Allen's Reptile Institute fell victim to the visitation freefall. Allen moved to the St. Augustine Alligator Farm for a spell, toyed with a couple of small ventures, and then teamed up with a former president of the Florida Herpetological Society to plan Ross Allen's Alligator Town. The fifty-acre attraction would include all the highlights of his reptile institute, including underwater alligator wrestling and a rattlesnake show. It would be perched just off I-75 near Lake City, and the idea was to grab tourists driving to and from Disney World. But Allen died a month before the planned June 1981 opening. He was seventy-three. The attraction still

opened, but it never had much sizzle. It finally closed around 2002.

One of Florida's earliest attractions to open—and close—was the Florida Ostrich Farm in Jacksonville. Begun soon after the St. Augustine Alligator Farm opened in the 1890s, it featured ostrich races and ostrich rides. Fluffy plumes for ladies' hats were also sold for large sums. But unlike many of Florida's alligator attractions, the ostrich farm closed because the bird races never rivaled the popularity of horse and dog races, and fashions changed regarding plumed hats.

Some tourist attractions died out because of a pre-Disney tourism shift away from certain regions, such as St. Petersburg. Still, Webb's City, the "world's most unusual drug store,"

Published by the Rotograph Company of New York, printed in Germany

1906 postcard of a streetcar stopping at Jacksonville's Florida Ostrich Farm.

flourished into the 1970s, having opened in 1925. Founder James Earl "Doc" Webb's philosophy was "Stack it high, sell it cheap," and this mind-set helped him to rapidly expand, even during the Great Depression. His store became more of an indoor mall or super Walmart, eventually covering seven city blocks with seventy-seven stores. Customers could buy anything from groceries to furniture to haircuts. Gimmicks and special attractions kept the store alive. There was rooftop dancing with Arthur Murray, breakfast for two cents, mermaids and chimp acts, and circus acts such as shooting a man out of a cannon.

Bill Hart was a credit manager for the store between 1966 and 1968.

The hours were long, 8 a.m. to 6 p.m. six days a week, but invariably something would happen that made you leave with a good story. . . . One day the lights went out and customers were asked to leave for their safety, but one woman, in the process of buying a bathing suit, refused to leave until she was told if the suit was dark blue or black.

The majority of the employees made minimum wage, but it helped many people make ends meet, including the five women working in my department. Four of those women had disabled husbands and the other was a single mother. Webb's also enabled many transients by hiring them to gather and return shopping carts to the stores. I'd see many of those people stop by the credit department to pick up their weekly check and would often never see them again.

At a time when Sunday business hours were not common,

Vintage postcard of Webb's City, postmarked 1951.

WEBB'S CITY, ST. PETERSBURG, FLORIDA

Published by Metrocraft Everett of Massachusetts; no copyright

Webb's City was open nearly every day of the year. On Christmas day we opened at noon, I'm told so the senior citizens would have a place to eat. Part of the hours of operation may have been with an eye on the bottom line, but I think "Doc" Webb also took care of his seniors who depended on him.

The scariest point in Hart's employment was when there was a threat of race riots in the area. "All department managers were told to report to work should a riot break out to help defend the stores," he said. "By defending the stores I'm referring to being given guns. Fortunately, that never happened, but it played a huge part in why I left to go to college."

Webb's closed its doors in 1977, but some of James Webb's innovations live on, such as the world's first express checkout line.

In the 1950s, Sunshine Springs near Sarasota was another attraction that tried to make its mark on the tourism world, drawing inspiration from Cypress Gardens and other attractions. It featured water-skiing shows with "the Aquabelles," tranquil boat rides through landscaped canals, and speedboats jumping through flaming hoops. It also featured a water-skiing elephant, Sunshine Sally, who belonged to the Ringling Bros. Circus. Never a real spring, the property and man-made lake were sold to a developer in 1960. "The place was quite remote then," said Marj Rusing, who skied with Sunshine Sally. "It was hard to get enough people to support the shows."

Many attractions faded, along with supporting businesses such as motels and restaurants, because they were bypassed by the interstate highway system. Unless they were conveniently located near an interstate exit, it was difficult to draw tourists from the much quicker routes. Many attractions tried to advertise as being on the way to Disney, virtually giving up on being a destination and content with serving as a temporary stopover point. And once Disney opened, several South Florida attractions suffered, since many tourists stopped venturing any farther south than the Orlando area, causing more economic ripples.

Some attractions died simply because their founders died first or became too ill to run them. They were usually small, one-person operations. Tom Gaskins's Cypress Knee Museum near Palmdale on U.S. 27 was one of those. Founded in 1951, the museum was a small building featuring unusual cypress knees, a shop selling polished knees, and a rickety boardwalk through a cypress swamp. A series of hand-lettered signs along the highway steered people to the attraction and appealed to their funny bone: "Come see Tom's Knees" and "Lady if he won't stop, hit him on the head with a shoe."

According to writer Jeff Klinkenberg, the main reason people visited the museum was to see Tom Gaskins himself. "What kind of a mood would he be in? Funny? Angry? Would he hanker to tell stories?" Klinkenberg wrote in *Seasons of Real Florida*. "He had interesting theories about staying healthy. He'd stand for hours on his head to increase the blood supply to his brain. Back when people thought exercise was to be avoided at all costs, he did hundreds of push-ups a day. Even when he was in his sixties he ran ten miles every morning along a creek, barefoot." Gaskins died in 1998, and his museum died soon afterward. His attraction embodied the term "sense of place" for South Florida's swamplands.

The many attractions that sank into oblivion for various reasons included Miracle Strip Amusement Park and the Snake-a-Torium in Panama City Beach, Florida Reptile Land in Lawtey (southwest of Jacksonville), Florida Ostrich Farm and Oriental Gardens in Jacksonville, Cross and Sword and Mystery House in St. Augustine, Jungle Gardens and Sea Zoo in Daytona Beach, Bongoland in Port Orange, Circus World and House of Mystery in Haines City, Mystery Fun House and Skull Kingdom in Orlando, Dupree Gardens near Land O' Lakes, Jungle Larry's Safari in Naples, Discovery Island and River Country in Lake Buena Vista, Masterpiece Gardens and Black Hills Passion Play in Lake Wales, Sanlando Springs in Longwood, Pirates World in Dania, Jungleland in Winter Haven, Texas Jim's Sarasota Reptile Farm and Zoo in Sarasota, and Black's Haunted House and Ocala Caverns in Ocala. A couple of websites, such as Florida's Lost Tourist Attractions and Florida Backroads Travel, keep a running tabulation. One website featuring bygone attractions stated that its pur-

pose was to pay "homage to the diversity that was Florida tourism."

As attractions faded, so did tourist associations such as the Tin Can Tourists of the World. The organization ceased to exist in 1977, although revival groups have sprung up and reunions with vintage rigs continue to

The Great Masterpiece attraction near Lake Wales (also known as Masterpiece Gardens) didn't survive the shift to Disney and other grander attractions, but neighboring Bok Tower Gardens did.

be held. Kampgrounds of America and the Good Sam Club, catering mostly to tourists who drive recreational vehicles, continue to exist.

In 1961, the national magazine *Travel USA* listed its top twelve tourist attractions in the country. Not surprisingly, three were in Florida: Silver Springs, Cypress Gardens, and Marineland of Florida. Today, most would list Disney World, Universal Studios, and SeaWorld as the top three, although there is a growing hunger for ecotourism venues and Old Florida–style attractions that differ from mainstream theme parks.

Of course, I don't miss some attractions. On my family's first trip to Florida in 1966, we stopped at our first Sunshine State roadside attraction. The zoo just south of Perry on U.S. 19 featured sad-looking animals in tiny cages on concrete floors, including a cramped Florida black bear that couldn't stand. We were disgusted and quickly left. The attraction is now closed, along with many like it.

Another closed attraction is the Lewis Plantation and Turpentine Still near Brooksville on U.S. 41, one of the Dixie Highway arteries. Created in 1935 by Pearce Lewis in response to declining revenues from his turpentine operations, he sought to turn his homestead into a *Gone with the Wind* Old South–style attraction, complete with African Americans who portrayed slaves. Happy slaves, I'm sure. Thankfully, changing attitudes eventually spelled its doom around 1981.

But before you think all of the fun, intriguing, and kitschy Old Florida tourist attractions have been lost, don't give in to melancholy. Many have survived, and others have morphed into something different and exciting, as we shall soon see.

Published by the Florida Attractions Association

"*Florida's Finest Attractions*" *brochure from the late 1950s before interstate highways in Florida. Only a handful of the featured attractions are now closed; most remain open in some form.*

PART III

OLD FLORIDA ATTRACTIONS YOU CAN VISIT

SIX

Florida to the Rescue

◇◇◇◇◇◇◇◇◇◇◇◇◇◇◇◇◇

As Disney World and other mega theme parks began to dominate the Florida tourist scene, almost three-quarters of the historical Florida attractions faded into memory. When some of the larger, most beloved attractions became threatened, concerned citizens sought help from the state of Florida to keep the gates open, and many of these efforts were successful.

HOMOSASSA SPRINGS

Ellie Schiller Homosassa Springs Wildlife State Park is located in Homosassa Springs on U.S. 19, seventy-five miles north of Tampa and ninety miles northwest of Orlando. Address: 4150 S. Suncoast Blvd. (U.S. 19), Homosassa, FL 34446; (352) 628-5343

Homosassa Springs has been a tourist attraction since the early 1900s, when it was a popular train stop. Passengers could picnic and take a dip in the spring while the cars were being loaded up with cedar, crabs, fish, and spring water. On a 1924 visit, Bruce Hoover of Chicago called the area "the most beautiful river and springs in the world." He bought land around the spring, founded the Homosassa Development Company, and built a bridge over the springs and two observatory decks. He called the spring a "natural bowl of fish," a description that would play into subsequent attempts to feature it.

In 1940, Elmo Reed and, later, professional angler David Newell became fascinated with the fact that both fresh- and saltwater fish species congregated in the spring bowl. An underwater dome was created where visitors could "walk underwater" beneath the spring's surface and watch the various fish and manatees swim about. The multitude of fish was astounding, numbering in the thousands—large jacks, snapper, snook, and others—all slowly swimming around the fish bowl. Thirty-four different fresh- and saltwater species have been identified. The attraction was called "Nature's Giant Fish Bowl," but the name was a bit of a misnomer. The fish were wild and free, looking in on the people who were inside the fish bowl!

Early Homosassa Springs brochure.

"Nature's Giant Fish Bowl," "the spring of 10,000 fish," remained a rather quaint attraction until the site was expanded into "Nature's Own Attraction" when purchased by the Norris Development Company in 1964. A zoo featuring native and exotic animals—including Lucifer (Lu) the Hippo—was established. Trained animals were housed at the springs when not in use for movies or television shows. Buck the Bear (known best for portraying Gentle Ben) was a popular feature. Alligator shows at the Gator Lagoon always drew a crowd since large gators would jump out of the water for fish and chicken. Monkey Landing featured a "barrel full of monkeys" because peanuts were tossed into a barrel for them to eat. Sea lions, goats, and chimps were also featured.

Wild but tame squirrels, fed by hand by visitors, were promoted as a special feature. A channel was dredged so visitors could be taken by boat from the visitor center along U.S. 19 to the

Fish circle the Homosassa Springs "Fish Bowl."

Contemporary Homosassa Springs sign showing "Indian maiden" shooting bow and arrow.

main zoo area and spring. And a new 180-ton floating "fish bowl," or underwater observatory, was built and slid into the springs using banana peels so as not to pollute the water with oil.

A tried-and-true marketing ploy was used that involved pretty young women for publicity photos. Instead of wearing bikinis, the women were dressed as mini-skirted Indian princesses, complete with black wigs. Perhaps it was because Homosassa was clearly an Indian word, one that means "a place where wild pepper grows" in the Seminole-Creek language.

Bruce Norris, owner of the company, planned to build a large city around the attraction, but a nationwide recession caused the company to dissolve. Canadian Pacific purchased the site and managed it for four years. When that company put it up for sale,

citizens convinced Citrus County to buy the attraction in 1984. Eventually, the attraction was sold to the state of Florida, where it became the Ellie Schiller Homosassa Springs Wildlife State Park in 1989. The park became a prime location for rehabilitating injured manatees, and a gate kept them inside the spring run.

True to the park service mission, an effort was made to remove exotic animals and plants, which included one of the original surviving animal stars: Lu the Hippo. Schoolchildren protested and started a letter-writing campaign, prompting then governor Lawton Chiles to declare Lu an honorary Florida citizen and therefore qualified for permanent housing at the park. As of January 2020, Lu was still going strong at Homosassa, entertaining visitors by opening his huge jaws while a volunteer tossed in cantaloupes, squash, and other vegetarian fare.

Born in 1960 at the San Diego Zoo and having had a long career as a celebrity animal actor in television and in movies beginning in 1964, Lu is vying to become the oldest hippo in captivity. Several other captive animals include a large alligator, black bears, red wolf, key deer, flamingoes, and whooping cranes. Most could not survive in the wild on their own, while some, such as injured black bears and otters, are being rehabilitated for eventual release. A Florida panther, brought to the park as an orphan at one week old, also roams a park enclosure.

Several free-ranging wild animals make use of the 210-acre park habitat, including black bears, herons, and egrets. As we have seen at several alligator attractions around the state, wading birds have established a rookery around the alligator habitat, since the reptiles discourage nest predation by raccoons and other creatures.

One thing remarkable about Homosassa is the love local residents have for the attraction. Park volunteers outnumber staff ten to one, and many of them worked at the attraction before state ownership. They do everything from interpretation to driving boats and trams. Visitor services would suffer without their help.

Lu the Hippo is fed by a volunteer at Homosassa.

Doug Alderson

WEEKI WACHEE SPRINGS

Weeki Wachee Springs State Park is located at the intersection of State Road 50 and U.S. 19, about twelve miles west of Brooksville. Address: 6131 Commercial Way, Weeki Wachee, FL 34606; (352) 592-5656

Just south of Homosassa is a sister attraction that primarily features human entertainment, one that pulls from the depths of mythology. Russians called them *rusalki*; the Japanese knew them as *ningyo*. To Scandinavians they were known as *margyr*; to the Australian Aboriginal people, *yawkyawks*. Cultures throughout the world have revered, admired, and fantasized about the mermaid. (Whether they were really oafish manatees tantalizing love-

Weeki Wachee mermaid statue.

Doug Alderson

sick sailors is beside the point.) The mermaid has long been part of our myth and culture. In 1946, Walton Hall Smith and Newt Perry keyed on that myth to create Florida's famous mermaid attraction at Weeki Wachee Springs. Although it wasn't the open ocean, the setting was breathtaking—a massive gin-clear spring with exposed limestone rock and a steep drop to a vent 185 feet deep, one of thirty-three Florida springs considered first magnitude. Promoters labeled it "The Mountain Underwater."

Weeki Wachee opened to the public on October 12, 1947, with local teens playing the mermaid roles but without the tails. Those came later, in the mid-1960s.

The initial mermaid tryouts weren't exactly rigorous, according to former mermaid Mary Darlington Fletcher in *Weeki Wachee: City of Mermaids* by Lu Vickers: "We lined up on the bank. Our test was to swim across the spring and back without drowning, and if we made it, and we all did, we were all mermaids all of a sudden." Perry was the tryout judge, and he preferred girls with long hair because of how the strands flowed underwater. Perry, Ricou Browning—who would become the original two-legged reptilian star in *Creature from the Black Lagoon*—and two women from Tallahassee whom

Postcard of Weeki Wachee mermaids "pre-tail."

Perry had trained at Wakulla Springs were charged with training the mermaids and creating the "underwater ballets." Perry developed breathing hoses, underwater breathing chambers, and even an underwater changing room. Initially, the first mermaids received hamburgers, hotdogs, and publicity but no pay. "When they'd get enough people for a show, we'd dive down thirty to thirty-five feet. When we were down on the bottom, it was sometimes scary because it was so cold, but we had a great time," said former mermaid Judy Ginty Cholomitis in *Weeki Wachee: City of Mermaids*.

U.S. 19 was a lonely two-lane highway when Weeki Wachee opened. Like mythological sirens, mermaids in their bathing suits lined the highway to lure drivers into the attraction. It often worked. Cypress Gardens and other attractions had already proven that

pretty young women drew in visitors, and many more attractions besides Weeki Wachee would follow.

The 1948 movie *Mr. Peabody and the Mermaid* was largely filmed at the springs. The attraction's performers assisted with the movie promotion, and it melded the mermaid image with Weeki Wachee to the present day.

The American Broadcasting Company (ABC) purchased the attraction in 1959 and made significant changes. It built the current one-of-a-kind four-hundred-seat theater sixteen feet below the spring's surface where visitors felt they were inside a flowing spring. Between shows, mermaids often posed atop a clamshell roof that could be seen from the highway, luring in visitors. ABC also installed large underwater props and created popular themes for the mermaid shows such as "Peter Pan," "Al-

A mermaid and a turtle in a Weeki Wachee performance.

Doug Alderson

Mermaids were instructed to follow several guidelines while performing: keep your head back, arch your back, keep your elbows straight, keep your fingers together, make slow circular pulls with your arms, keep the instep of your foot beside your knee, point your toes and force your foot outward so it doesn't turn in, and lock the knee in your straight leg. The last instruction simply said, "Do all of these things at the same time." And, oh, yes, hold your breath for long periods of time, smile a lot, and don't look cold in the frigid 74-degree spring water.

A 1953 advertisement for mermaids in the *St. Petersburg Times* painted a rosy picture of the job: "Weeki Wachee, Spring of the Mermaids, has openings for two girl swimmers in our world famous Mermaid Troupe. Pleasant working conditions, assured advancement, year-round employment with our congenial company. All expenses paid during training period starting soon. You MUST be a good swimmer, in good health. Age 18–25. Write your swimming qualifications and send a snapshot, preferably in swimming suit. Personal interview will follow." Surprisingly, some applicants had poor swimming skills and had to be rescued during tryouts. Perhaps they believed the mermaid magic would somehow transform them.

ice in Wonderland," "Snow White," and "The Wizard of Oz." By the early 1960s, the eight shows a day were often sold out, and up to half a million visitors a year came from all over the United States and the world. The thirty-five mermaids employed there were treated like celebrities wherever they went. Tryouts were competitive and drew applicants from five continents. And the spring was so clear on most days that some visitors and viewers claimed the shows weren't real, especially when seen in movies, television shows, and advertisements.

Weeki Wachee reached its peak during the mid-1960s. Then along came I-75. It began to siphon travelers from U.S. 19. Weeki Wachee suffered, but a nearby attraction just to the north, Fort Dodge, was hit harder. Fort Dodge opened in 1962 and was another faux

Old West town that had a unique feature—the Old Salty Mine. Visitors could pan for gold, silver nuggets, and semiprecious stones in a three-hundred-foot stream. The mine and town closed four years after it opened.

During its heyday, Weeki Wachee also featured an "abandoned Seminole village" that was a stop on a "covered wagon" tram ride. Visitors could wander through the thatched huts known as chickees, view authentic dugout canoes, and ponder what had happened to the occupants. The attraction saved money by not hiring Seminoles to occupy the village as at Silver Springs. Around the time visitation began to plummet, a forest fire burned the village, and it was never rebuilt.

Another feature at Weeki Wachee, the May Museum of the Tropics, which boasted a giant statue of a Her-cules beetle and "the largest, most bizarre collection of arthropods in the nation," closed around the same period and moved to Colorado Springs, oversized beetle and all. One reason was environmental. Even though Florida was a great place for living bugs, its infamous summer humidity was not kind to preserved specimens.

Even ABC's deep pockets couldn't stop the changing tourism demographics. The corporation sold both Weeki Wachee and Silver Springs to Leisure Attractions in 1984. In 1999, Leisure Attractions unloaded Weeki Wachee to the Weeki Wachee Springs Company, which in turn donated

Mold-A-Matic machine at Weeki Wachee Springs State Park, one of the last ones in operation at Florida attractions.

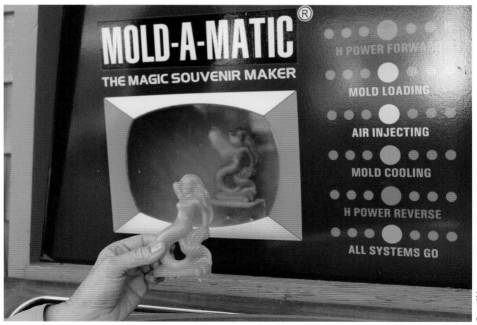

it to the town of Weeki Wachee—population twelve—four years later for a tax credit. "The Only City with Live Mermaids," as the town bills itself, began a desperate "Save Our Tails" campaign led by former mermaid and elected mayor Robyn Anderson, a self-described "mer-mayor." Eventually, state ownership followed, and Florida's 160th state park opened in 2008. Former mermaids, whose motto is "Once a mermaid, always a mermaid," are still active with the attraction, and the periodic Mermaids of Yesteryear shows are often sold out. Current and former mermaids describe working at the attraction as a "sisterhood" where everyone knows each other's business and lifelong friendships are made.

As boys, my brother and I begged our parents to take us to Weeki Wachee, but the closest we got in 1966 was the parking lot. We pulled in, gawked at the topless concrete mermaid statues, and my parents thought better of it. It wasn't until 2010 that I fulfilled my dream as a mature adult. I quietly laughed the entire time. The mermaid show was hugely entertaining, campy Old Florida, and I admired the stamina and athleticism of the mermaid performers. A mermaid performer once said that diving into the strong current of the spring was like trying to swim up a waterfall. It took fortitude, and the performers had to smile and make it look effortless while performing an elaborate underwater ballet. Not surprisingly, today's mermaids have to be scuba certified.

What stole the show during my initial visit was a small slider turtle doing back flips as if to imitate the mermaids. After all, this was the turtle's spring; the mermaids came much later in the historical timeline of such things. Some shows are interrupted by a visiting manatee. Author Lu Vickers aptly described Weeki Wachee as "a collision of kitsch and nature."

How long the mermaid performances will last is anyone's guess, but for now I revel in the fact that Weeki Wachee still has its mermaids thanks to the state of Florida. About thirty

A Weeki Wachee mermaid waves good-bye.

mermaids are employed at the park; of these, several are often on the road promoting Weeki Wachee at venues around the country. They do four daily shows during the summer and three a day after Labor Day. And they have a friend in singer Jimmy Buffet. He watched the mermaids perform at age seven, and they made a lifelong impression. He now posts videos of performing mermaids on a giant screen at his concerts while he sings "Mermaid in the Night," and sometimes a contingent of Weeki Wachee mermaids will join him onstage, pulled on a cart since they can't walk while wearing the tails. The extra attention may have contributed to rising park attendance in recent years. One reporter called it "a Buffet bump." After all, Weeki Wachee is still the only mermaid theater in the world.

RAINBOW SPRINGS

Rainbow Springs State Park is located three miles north of Dunnellon on the east side of U.S. 41. The Campground, Tube Area, and Headspring each have a separate entrance. Address: 19158 SW 81st Place Rd., Dunnellon, FL 34432; (352) 465-8555

Less than an hour's drive to the east of Weeki Wachee, Rainbow Springs near Dunnellon began the transformation from local hangout to famous tourist attraction when Frank Greene and F. E. Hemphill took over the springs in 1937. The first step was changing the name from Blue Springs to Rainbow Springs

An early postcard featuring one of the Rainbow Springs "underwater boats."

Published by the Hicks News Agency, Inc., of Ocala; no copyright

and the spring run from Blue Run to the Rainbow River. It proved to be a brilliant move. While there are several Blue Springs in the state of Florida, Rainbow Springs was a new moniker, and it conjured up a multifaceted jewel of color. A lodge and tourist cabins were built, and a glass-bottom boat known as the *Rainbow Queen* carried passengers downriver. But two additions separated Rainbow Springs from similar attractions. One was a man-made waterfall known as Rainbow Falls—"the only scenic waterfall in Florida." The other was the "submarine boats." These were half submerged, and visitors were able to sit below the water line and view the spring's wonders from a unique vantage point.

In the 1950s, Rainbow Springs was owned by the same company that owned Rock City near Chattanooga. And as was the case with its sister attraction, "See Rainbow Springs" advertisements were painted on barns, especially along U.S. 41 through Georgia. Attendance at the attraction hit a plateau on Independence Day in 1965, when combined ticket sales for the submarine boats and glass-bottom boats topped $1,000. A year later, however, the new I-75 was carrying nearly three times more tourists than U.S. 19, 27, 441, and 41 combined. Still, the attraction hung on for several more years as extra features were added to make the eighteen-mile drive from I-75 more worthwhile. The Leaf Ride monorail, featuring leaf-shaped gondolas, was added in the late 1960s along with a magnificent fountain with a rainbow backdrop. Simulated log rafts on the river added a more rustic experience for visitors.

Hollywood breathed new life into the attraction in the summer of 1971 when it was announced that scenes for *Tarzan and the Brown Prince* would be filmed at the springs. In one scene, Tarzan actor Steve Hawkes (aka Steve Sipek) was to be burned at the stake. Fiction turned into gruesome reality when too much gasoline was added to the wet leaves, and the fire raged out of control. The film crew fled, ignoring Hawkes's screams, but a lion actor refused to leave. Hawkes recalled the life-changing event: "I was burned over ninety percent of my body. And guess who saved my life? A Lion named Samson. He dragged me out of the burning fire and ripped off the ropes I was staked down with. Then I realized what the animals were all about."

Since the film crew ran from the fire and left him to die, Hawkes turned his back on acting, eventually moved to Loxahatchee, Florida, in rural Palm Beach County, and started a sanctuary for mistreated lions, tigers, cougars, and leopards. "The love that I have for them cannot be measured by anything that life offers," he said. "God did not put animals on this earth to be killed, nor man to hunt them down and enjoy their agonies as they die. That's why if there ever was such a man as Tarzan, I'm probably the closest one to him." Hawkes eventually ran afoul of state captive-animal regulations, and his big cats were removed. He passed away in 2019, and his two remaining big cats are being cared for at the Mystic Jungle Educational Facility near Live Oak.

Ownership of Rainbow Springs changed several times, but despite new ideas and features, the attraction closed in 1974, and the infrastructure fell into disrepair. Local citizens eventually organized to seek public ownership, and the state of Florida purchased Rainbow Springs in 1990. It opened as a state park in 1995 with great fanfare, the keynote speaker being *Rainbow Queen* captain Dave Edwards. However, many of the old features, such as the monorail and submarine boats, were not salvageable. And like many golden age attractions that were adopted by the state, increased emphasis was placed on conservation and nature-based recreation. Park officials selectively chose to continue viable commercial enterprises that were compatible with the state park mission.

DE LEON SPRINGS

De Leon Springs State Park is located about six miles north of Deland off U.S. 17. Turn west onto Ponce de Leon Boulevard and travel one mile to the entrance of the park. Address: 601 Ponce de Leon Blvd., De Leon Springs, FL 32130; (386) 985-4212

De Leon Springs near Deland was once called Acuera, or "Healing Waters," by Timucuan Indians who had inhabited the area for millennia before being largely wiped out by disease and warfare in the 1700s. William Williams called it "Spring Garden" in 1804 when he obtained it from a Spanish land grant.

Naturalist John James Audubon visited the springs in 1831. "This spring presents a circular basin, having a diameter of about sixty feet, from the centre of which the water is thrown up with great force, although it does not rise to a height of more than a few inches above the general level," he wrote in his journal. "A kind of whirlpool is formed, on the edges of which are deposited vast quantities of shells, with pieces of wood, gravel, and other substances, which have co-alesced into solid masses having a very curious appearance."

A sugar cane mill was soon constructed at the springs, utilizing the huge volume of water gushing forth. The mill was destroyed by Seminoles in 1835, rebuilt, and destroyed again by Union troops during the Civil War, when it was being used to grind corn for the Confederacy. It is believed that the mill was restored again in the late 1800s during a time when visitors were brought in by steamboat from the St. Johns River. The name changed to De Leon Springs in 1886 after a railroad depot and winter resort were built. The new name, after the early Spanish explorer Juan Ponce de León, gave the spring a mythical "Fountain of Youth" connotation to sound more appealing to northern visitors. A small resort emerged, and an inn and casino were

Liz Dane performing with Queenie during a De Leon Springs performance.

built in the 1920s. This development was followed by the establishment of a larger attraction that featured a water-skiing elephant in the 1950s and early 1960s.

Queenie the elephant stood on a raft with skis beside Marj Rusing, formerly of Sunshine Springs, as part of a water circus. She was closely followed by a young woman named Liz Dane. Dane also did circus acts on land with Queenie. "My Dad [Bill Green] was hired by the owner of Ponce de Leon Springs, Lee Norwood, to bring his trained animals to the park to put on shows for the park's visitors," said Dane. "The trained animals included the elephant, Queenie, a zebra, miniature Sicilian donkeys, a dog and two monkeys, and six llamas."

Liz Dane gives Queenie a hug during a visit to Queenie's retirement home at Wild Adventures in Georgia, April 2006.

The attraction also offered jungle cruises that took visitors past "Old Methuselah," an ancient bald cypress tree, and to an island full of monkeys. When business turned sour, the state purchased the springs, which became a state park in 1982.

Queenie, the water-skiing elephant, was sold by Liz Dane's family in 1967, and she eventually retired to Wild Adventures near Valdosta, Georgia, where she died in 2011. Liz Dane was able to track her down in 2005 and wrote this about their meeting:

> Unfortunately, when with the circus in California, Queenie developed a huge distrust of people, especially strangers, and would just as soon bat a stranger with her trunk as look at them. So, Kurt [the head elephant keeper at Wild Adventures] was a bit apprehensive to let me get too close to Queenie as he was not sure what she would do. She stopped about half way to me, so Kurt went over to Queenie and reassured her that all was okay.
>
> When I first saw her, I spoke her name and she immediately showed signs of some level of recognition. Her ears went out and she started slowly walking toward me. I continued to talk to her and she eventually came close enough to smell my hands and my feet. There was still a heavy cabled fence between us; however, Kurt felt there were enough positive signs of recognition that it would be safe for us to get closer. So we walked around to the other side of the enclosure, came thru the elephant barn and ended up right inside the enclosure with Queenie.
>
> She came right up to me and it was like we had never been apart. I cried! She just stood there touching me with her trunk and rumbling, which would be equitable to a cat purring. In other words, a sound of contentment.

After that first visit, Dane visited her elephant friend several more times.

The original mill at De Leon Springs was slated for destruction in 1961, but Peter Schwarze stepped in to restore it for the one-of-a-kind Old Spanish Sugar Mill Restaurant. The mill is now electrically powered to grind flour, and the eatery is famous for the grills at each table. For generations, people

Doug Alderson

You can make your own pancakes at your table at the Old Spanish Sugar Mill Restaurant.

A busy morning at the Old Spanish Sugar Mill Restaurant.

Doug Alderson

have lined up to get a turn at making their own pancakes, eggs, and sausage. It's as close to home cooking as you can get away from home. Besides the usual unbleached white flour, there is a stone-ground mixture of five different flours, and with all the pancake additions that can be ordered—blueberries, bananas, peanut butter, pecans, chocolate chips, apples, and applesauce—people get very creative. Laughter frequently erupts from the tables. The restaurant is busy and loud, especially on weekends. The service is fast, and the meal a bit messy and wonderful. And you don't have dishes to clean up!

SILVER SPRINGS

Silver Springs State Park is located about five miles east of Ocala on State Road 40 just past the intersection with State Road 35. Address: 5656 E. Silver Springs Blvd., Ocala, FL 34488; (352) 236-7148

Florida's most famous springs attraction, Silver Springs, held on the longest as a private attraction. But interstate highways, Disney World, and other mega theme parks in the Orlando area had a growing impact. After the property suffered a slow death from a business standpoint,

Published by the Rotograph Company of New York and printed in Germany

Postcard image of glass-bottom rowboat at Silver Springs, circa 1906.

Kayakers and a glass-bottom boat float over the main boil at Silver Springs.

Doug Alderson

the Florida Park Service took control of it in early 2013. "Silver Springs is special and represents 'Old Florida,'" said then Florida Park Service director Donald Forgione at the opening. "I look forward to protecting it and helping people enjoy and appreciate all that it offers."

Some changes were made. Admission prices were reduced to reflect those of other state parks. The zoo was phased out. The water park was in disrepair and was eventually torn down. Willie Nelson gave the first big concert at the new park, and at Christmas there was a popular laser light show. The glass-bottom boats continued to run with veteran boat captains, and, for the first time, canoes and kayaks could be launched near the headsprings area.

For the same admission, visitors could also access the state land across the river—formerly known as Silver River State Park—and enjoy hiking, off-road bicycling, and horseback riding. A campground and rental cabins became available, and one could visit the pioneer Cracker village and Silver River Museum and Environmental Education Center.

The best way to view the depths of the various springs at Silver Springs is to take a glass-bottom boat ride. Although the springs have suffered from decreased flow levels and increased nitrate levels, which have caused algae growth, the clarity of the water is still impressive, depending on recent rainfall in the area. On most days, Silver Springs is a kaleidoscope of refracting light.

WAKULLA SPRINGS

Wakulla Springs is located about fifteen miles south of Tallahassee. Take U.S. 319 south and bear left at State Road 61. Travel six miles and turn left onto State Road 267 at the flashing stoplight. Take an immediate right into the park entrance. Address: 465 Wakulla Park Dr., Wakulla Springs, FL 32327; (850) 561-7276

Swimming is ever popular at Wakulla Springs, fifteen miles south of Tallahassee. Though Wakulla Springs was never a mega attraction like Silver Springs, perhaps due to a lack of other nearby attractions to keep tourists busy for a multiday visit, glass-bottom boat tours began circling the massive spring bowl in 1925 when real-estate developer George T. Christie purchased the spring.

The springs area was more intensely developed as a resort when it was purchased by millionaire businessman Ed Ball in 1934. He also came to own four thousand acres of surrounding property. A brother-in-law of Alfred I. DuPont, Ball owned the Florida East Coast Railroad, Florida National Bank, and the St. Joe Paper Company. He viewed the springs more as a personal retreat than as a

Published by the Albertype Company of Brooklyn, New York; no copyright

1943 postcard of alligator tour boat at Wakulla Springs.

moneymaking operation, building an ornate Mediterranean-style lodge overlooking the spring that boasted only thirty-seven rooms. Ball's private room occupied the upstairs corner and was the only one with bars on the windows. With his many business dealings and a highly contentious divorce, Ball had made enemies.

To promote Wakulla Springs, Ball hired Newton Perry as his manager in 1937. Perry had numerous Hollywood contacts and began filming underwater promos and skits. He developed underwater air stations and air hoses that he would later use and refine at Weeki Wachee Springs, and it has been surmised that the routines of the visiting Tarpon Club Synchronized Swimming Team from the Florida State College for Women in Tallahassee gave Perry ideas for the Weeki Wachee mermaids. Several movies were filmed at the springs, too. Johnny Weissmuller, a former Olympic swimmer and the

Published by Curteich-Chicago; no copyright

Postcard from 1946 showing Newt Perry and one of the underwater air stations he developed at Wakulla Springs.

most famous of the Tarzan actors, was featured in parts of two movies filmed at the springs—*Tarzan's Secret Treasure* and *Tarzan's New York Adventure*. Parts of *Creature from the Black Lagoon*, *Airport 77*, and *Joe Panther* were also filmed at the springs.

Ricou Browning went from Wakulla Springs lifeguard to Hollywood actor when he ended up doing the underwater scenes as the creature in *Creature from the Black Lagoon* due to his ability to hold his breath for several minutes and ably swim wearing the heavy reptilian suit. During one long filming episode on a raft in the middle of the springs, he began swimming to shore wearing the costume but without the headgear so he could walk to the hotel to use the restroom. "I noticed at the diving tower that the ladder goes up to the walkway and there was a woman with a little girl," he said in a 2003 interview at the Wakulla Springs "Creaturefest." "I didn't think anything of it, and I came up to the ladder to climb up. And as I climbed out, of course I revealed the suit. And this little girl was scared to death. She started running down the walkway, and her mother behind her, and I jumped up all the way, and started saying, 'Hey wait a minute, I'm not a monster!' And the more I did that, the more frightened the little girl was."

Browning went on to star in and assist with several other movies, and he credits Ed Ball with protecting Wakulla Springs: "He saved this place, I think, for what it is. If he hadn't done that . . . we'd probably see a bunch of houses around here. . . . I think there are a lot of Florida stories that are written and can be told, but there's no place to shoot 'em but here. Cause there's no other places that still look like what Florida looked like when it began, so to speak."

Don Gavin, a veteran boat driver at the springs, remembered Ball well: "He'd often take friends and business associates on boat rides and I'd be the driver. Mr. Ball would always give me a dollar tip, but one day he gave me two dollars. I was surprised and pleased, but Mr. Ball walked up the hill a ways, stopped, turned around and came back. 'Did I give you two dollars?' he asked. 'Yes Sir, you did.' 'Well, two bills must have been stuck together.' So, he took that extra dollar back."

Tallahassee Democrat editor Malcolm Johnson complained about lost economic opportunity at the springs under Ball's ownership. "It stays open more by a wealthy owner's sufferance than by paid attendance," he lamented in 1963.

In 1941, Ball erected a controversial fence across the Wakulla River 4.5 miles below the springs to keep out boaters so his jungle and glass-bottom boats could run unfettered. While the fence—and Ball's dredging activities in the upper basin—eventually brought on a legal challenge in the early 1970s, Ball's fence remained.

Ball died in 1981, and ownership of the springs fell to Alfred DuPont's Nemours Foundation, which put it up for sale. Many feared a developer would take over the property, so, after much public outcry, the state purchased the springs in 1986. "The Wakulla Springs acquisition was especially significant because with it came not only one of the world's most impressive fresh water springs, but also an essentially complete public use complex, including an architecturally appealing 27-room lodge," wrote then Florida Park Service superintendent Ney Landrum in *Legacy of Green*. "The property had long been sought for a state park—at one time with the hope that it might even be donated—but when it was actually in hand it created some new management challenges for the Park Service, which had never operated a hostelry or major dining facility before."

The Edward Ball Wakulla Springs State Park continued the boat operations and kept the lodge open, leasing it to various concessionaires over time. And the state followed in the tradition of not putting televisions in the rooms, in keeping with the 1930s appearance. Period furniture and the original elevators remain, along with the incredible painted ceilings in the lobby that depict birds and Spanish and Florida scenes. Visitors can gaze upon the painted ceiling or play a game of checkers on a marble checkerboard. The whole idea is to slow down and enjoy a relaxed pace of life.

The Wakulla River fence stayed in place, too, and few today argue for its removal. The section of river just upstream of the fence is probably the most undisturbed of any navigable waterway in Florida. The only human intrusions are when state biologists periodically canoe the section to count the many alligators and wading birds.

For several years after state purchase of the springs, Wakulla Springs remained as clear as in this 1921 description by John Faris: "The water is so clear that a small stone lying on the bottom, much more than one hundred feet below the surface, can be distin-

Inside the Wakulla Springs Lodge.

Doug Alderson

Wakulla Springs park ranger Don Gavin, photographed in 2012. Gavin passed away in 2017.

Doug Alderson

guished easily. In fact, the waters act as a magnifying glass; they are convex at the surface because of the rapid boiling up from the hidden outlet of a stream that flows a long distance in a channel deep underground. From the spring the water flows to the Gulf in a stream so large that large boats float on it with ease."

By the late 1990s, the water emerging from Wakulla Springs became increasingly murky for a variety of reasons, including sea-level rise and groundwater pumping in the region. This change affected the running of glass-bottom boats, but the Wakulla Springs jungle boat rides are ever popular, with plenty of big alligators, wading birds, and manatees to see. And visitors revel in a lodge that seems little changed from its historical appearance, all thanks to the state of Florida.

SEVEN

The American Alligator Keeps On Giving

◇◇◇◇◇◇◇◇◇◇◇◇◇◇◇◇

"Drawing on scientific observation, speculation, imagination, exaggeration, affection, fear, historic resources, artistic inspiration, hunger, and economic motivation, Americans have found an astounding number of ways of integrating the alligator into their lives. It has become symbol, totem, medicine, mascot, pet, handbag, saddle, main dish, hors d'oeuvre, nightmare and souvenir."

Vaughn L. Glasgow, *A Social History
of the American Alligator* (1991)

"There is a primeval vibe to Florida. An unambiguous sense of nature's supremacy. It is there in the tides and the ball-bearing rains and the insects as big as snowshoes and the vines that never stop growing. Florida feels, amid the heavy green and wet, as if it could overtake you at any moment. Alligators make sense here."

Allison Glock, *"The Gator Wrestlers,"
Garden & Gun* (2008)

Almost every roadside attraction during Florida's golden age of tourism seemed to have large alligators in cages or "alligator pits," and alligators even pulled carts of children at some places. Even today's Florida Citrus Centers along the interstates feature monster stuffed alligators and live baby alligators in tanks. Florida visitors never seem to tire of seeing large-toothed reptiles up close—but from a safe vantage point—as proven by the state's many successful alligator attractions. And these attractions have diversified in recent years, adding such things as zip lines and bird watching to broaden their appeal.

Top: A vintage postcard, postmarked 1905, showing a couple paddling an alligator like a canoe. Bottom: Past attractions even had harnessed alligators pulling children in carts.

GATORLAND

Gatorland is located on U.S. 441 just north of Kissimmee. The easiest way to reach it is to turn west onto State Road 417 from the Florida Turnpike and then take an immediate left onto U.S. 441. Address: 14501 S. Orange Blossom Trl., Orlando, FL 32837; (407) 855-5496 or (800) 393-5297

Mike Hileman has many roles at Kissimmee's Gatorland—alligator wrestler, entertainment coordinator, and director of adventure programs—but a new task was recently bestowed upon him that stands in stark contrast to the others: Hileman is also the attraction's bird sanctuary manager. That's because the attraction, begun by the late Owen Godwin in 1949, is home each year to several hundred nesting wading birds, including wood storks (which until 2014 were listed as an endangered species) and roseate spoonbills.

Fresh from wrestling an alligator for an appreciative crowd, Hileman took me on a tour of the bird rookery area. We followed a boardwalk that stretches around a swamp and lagoon and ends at a three-story viewing tower. It was a slow walk because tiny openings in thick foliage provided glimpses of several active bird nests. In one spot, several fuzzy-headed baby egrets were poking up their heads in anticipation of their parents' arrival with food. It's no wonder that Gatorland was added as a stop on the

The author at the Gatorland entrance.

Steve Alderson

Mike Hileman on the boardwalk at the Gatorland bird sanctuary.

Doug Alderson

Doug Alderson

state-sponsored Great Florida Birding and Wildlife Trail in 2000.

Hileman explained that in 1991, the year he started working at the 110-acre facility, Frank Godwin opened up this back slough area as a natural breeding marsh for alligators. He predicted that wading birds would follow. The results? There were two little green heron nests that first year, seven the next year, and then, the year after that, more species than they could count. "They've been coming ever since," said Hileman. "He [Godwin] just knew the way of the wilds."

According to Hileman, the birds came for two reasons: habitat and protection. "This place is an oasis amid urban sprawl," he said. "We have wetlands and almost thirty acres that are untouched. We also have a lot of alligators. They protect the nests from predators such as raccoons, opossums,

An assortment of wading birds at Gatorland, including wood storks, white ibises, and snowy egrets.

bobcats, and snakes, even though they eat an occasional bird. It's a symbiotic relationship. The same thing happens in the wild."

The total number of wading birds now rivals the more than thirteen hundred alligators and eighty crocodiles found at Gatorland. So, how does all this relate to tourism and business survivability?

Word is spreading among bird lovers about Gatorland's breeding marsh and colony because it is one of the largest and most accessible colonies in Florida. Visitors can easily view the feeding, courtship, mating, and nest-

Close-up of one of the prehistoric-looking wood storks at Gatorland.

Doug Alderson

ing behaviors of both alligators and wading birds, since the animals have become accustomed to people. Early-entry and late-departure passes are available so photographers and bird watchers can take advantage of better lighting and fewer crowds. And all of this means extra revenue for the attraction. It's part of a long line of innovations the attraction has introduced over the years.

Gatorland, billed as central Florida's first tourist attraction, started as a sixteen-acre borrow pit created to build Highways 17/92 and 441 and purchased by Godwin and two other investors for $300. Godwin filled it with alligators. Locals thought him crazy since alligators could easily be seen in the wild. He soon added a huge array of snakes and a Seminole Indian village.

In the 1950s, to keep visitors coming, Godwin purchased a giant fifteen-foot crocodile known as Bone Crusher and billed it as the world's largest captive crocodile; he also featured a twelve-foot alligator he called Cannibal Jake. He took both on the road, and the money collected helped to keep the attraction afloat, as well as providing much needed advertising.

The 1960s proved more lucrative as Godwin added African animals. In 1962, the famous concrete gaping gator jaw was built at the attraction's entrance. In 1965, a train was added—much to the delight of visiting children. The 1970s marked two milestones: the premier of a two-thousand-foot boardwalk known as the Swamp Walk and the beginning of research into alligator reproduction. Gatorland is the only place in the world where alligators have successfully been artificially inseminated.

Adjoining land was purchased in the 1980s, and Gatorland continued to expand its size and scope through the 1990s, adding an eight-hundred-seat Gator Wrestling Stadium, a larger train tour, and the alligator breeding marsh that would ultimately attract breeding wading birds as well. Four

Gatorland alligator wrestler Avi shows off a classic move.

Doug Alderson

of the world's largest white "leucistic" alligators were added in 2009, and in 2011 the park completed the $1.8 million Screamin' Gator Zip Line for high-flying thrills.

Besides the innovations and adaptability to changing times and visitor desires, Gatorland is likely one of the few Old Florida–style attractions to have benefited from Disney's arrival, since the mega theme park and others that followed brought millions more tourists to the area. Godwin's original choice of location proved fortuitous. And perhaps another reason the family-owned attraction has survived and thrived is its ability to cultivate talent like Mike Hileman.

Hileman started his stint at the popular attraction working at the Gatorland restaurant in 1991, but in less than two months he was learning the art of "Florida Cracker-style" alligator wrestling. "They treat you like family here," he said. "You're not just a number."

The wrestling techniques were brought to Gatorland by employee Tim Williams, who learned from renowned reptile expert and showman Ross Allen at Silver Springs and later at the St. Augustine Alligator Farm Zoological Park.

"Edutainment is our goal," Hileman said. "The public won't sit still for a lecture, so we try to educate people while entertaining them."

JUNGLE ADVENTURES

Jungle Adventures is located on State Road 50 about fifteen miles east of Orlando. Address: 26205 E. Colonial Dr., Christmas, FL 32709; (407) 568-2885

Alligators are a key ingredient in the survivability of many other attractions besides Gatorland. That includes Jungle Adventures in tiny Christmas between Orlando and Titusville, one of the newest, with roots dating back to 1989. Jungle Adventures boasts the world's largest man-made alligator, Swampy. At two hundred feet, it is large enough to house the attraction's ticket counter, gift shop, and offices.

The attraction features a host of critters, including panthers, bears, wolves, tropical birds, and, of course, very large alligators as part of a "timeless old Florida Hidden Treasure attraction on a journey into a lost world that time forgot," according to the website. A Jungle Swamp Cruise in which visitors are "surrounded by more than 200 alligators" and the Gator Jamboree Feeding are two highlights.

EVERGLADES ATTRACTIONS: Billie Swamp Safari and Gator Park Airboat Tours

The easiest way to reach Billie Swamp Safari is to take Alligator Alley (I-75) from either the west or the east to Exit 49, about halfway between Naples and Fort Lauderdale. Head north about sixteen miles, following signs to the Big Cypress Reservation. Signs point the way. Address: 30000 Gator Tail Trl., Clewiston, FL 33440; (863) 983-6101

Gator Park Airboat Tours in the Everglades near Miami features alligator wrestling, baby alligators that visitors can hold, exotic birds, lots of snakes, and airboat tours deep into the Everglades. Airboat tours to see wild alligators are common along the Tamiami Trail (U.S. 41) west of Miami and at Billie Swamp Safari on the Big Cypress Seminole Indian Reservation.

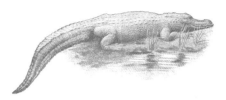

ST. AUGUSTINE ALLIGATOR FARM ZOOLOGICAL PARK

The St. Augustine Alligator Farm Zoological Park is located just a few miles south of St. Augustine on State Road A1A (Anastasia Boulevard). Address: 999 Anastasia Blvd., St. Augustine, FL 32080; (904) 824-3337

Florida's longest-running alligator attraction is the St. Augustine Alligator Farm. In the late 1800s, George Reddington and Felix Fire were conductor and fireman, respectively, on a train running from St. Augustine to St. Augustine Beach. Passengers often marveled at basking alligators, and the train frequently stopped so Reddington and Fire could move alligators from the tracks. One day, they decided to gather up alligators and put them in a bathhouse on the beach, charging visitors a quarter for a look. Their success inspired them to start the St. Augustine Alligator Farm at South Beach on Anastasia Island in 1893.

"Gawking ticket holders shuddered with delicious late-Victorian horror at pool banks piled high with basking saurians, and they shared vicarious shivers with friends and neighbors back home by sending them outrageous Edwardian-era postcards of alligator hordes and alligator atrocities," wrote Vaughn Glasgow in *A Social History of the American Alligator*.

Besides offering entertainment, the farm and several copycat attractions sold a variety of alligator leather goods and teeth, stuffed alligators, postcards that were often doctored, and the ever-popular live baby alligators. Thousands of babies were sold each year, and if they ran short, several outlets imported baby caimans from Central America. So many were brought up north that in 1943 the Chicago Zoological Park complained of having four to five hundred live alligators of

Alligators at the St. Augustine Alligator Farm Zoological Park.

Doug Alderson

varying lengths on hand. They desperately tried to ship some back south for reintroduction. Today, regulations concerning the sale and ownership of baby alligators vary from state to state, and reports of escaped or released pet alligators in northern cities such as Pittsburgh are numerous.

The St. Augustine Alligator Farm flourished until 1920, when a fierce nor'easter washed out the railroad tracks to South Beach, isolating the attraction. Subsequent fires prompted a move closer to the St. Augustine hotels and historical lighthouse on Anastasia Island, where it remains today. Ownership changed hands in 1937 to W. I. Drysdale and F. Charles Usina. Drysdale and Usina expanded the attraction and succeeded in attracting international attention. In the 1970s, when ownership was turned over to

Drysdale's son, David, the attraction changed from roadside attraction to an accredited zoo and conservation facility. Scientists from the University of Florida conducted alligator research at the facility, with the best known being a thesis about the courtship habits of alligators.

The Alligator Farm's Land of Crocodiles opened in 1993 and featured all twenty-three of the world's crocodile species—a first for any facility. As part of its breeding program, some rare Chinese alligators raised at the park were fitted with transmitters and returned to the wild in China. And, as in the evolution of Gatorland, a bird rookery for wading birds emerged and expanded to more than six hundred nests, much to the delight of birdwatchers and wildlife photographers. Great egret nesting begins in February

The massive stuffed body of Gomek, one of the world's largest saltwater crocodiles, once entertained visitors at the St. Augustine Alligator Farm Zoological Park.

Doug Alderson

around Valentine's Day, with wood storks beginning to arrive later that month. Snowy egrets, little blue herons, tricolored herons, roseate spoonbills, and green herons round out the nesting in late March and April. By July, fledgling birds are everywhere.

"That's the most Mother Nature we have here," said reptile curator Jim Darlington. "I saw photos in birding magazines and I would recognize the tree." The facility sells special photo passes that allow for early entry and late departure to take advantage of ideal lighting and bird activity. "Sometimes, they line up along the boardwalk and it looks like the sidelines of an NFL game," Darlington said with a laugh.

The Crocodile Crossing zip line was installed in 2011 to enable visitors to view alligators and crocodiles from a new perspective, often directly over

their pools. "That's the funnest thing to do in St. Augustine," said Darlington. "When the course first opened, I would feed them [alligators and crocodiles] from above to get them to look up when people are going over. But they soon became desensitized to people on the course because they weren't feeding them." During my visit, there were no reptilian beasts gazing skyward with jaws agape while humans were doing their high-wire act, but I gathered that it was still an added thrill for participants. "I'm sure it can be fun zip-lining over a parking lot," said Darlington. "But going over crocodiles and alligators, that's an added extra."

The attraction is now called the St. Augustine Alligator Farm Zoological Park to reflect changes over the last few decades. "The St. Augustine Alli-

A Crocodile Crossing zip line participant at the St. Augustine Alligator Farm Zoological Park.

Doug Alderson

A gharial, native to India, is one of the various species of crocodiles, alligators, and other reptiles at the zoological park.

Doug Alderson

gator Farm has never actually acted as an alligator farm," said director John Bruegger. "It started with a lot of American alligators, and I think it was attractive to think of it as a farm. Nowadays the term 'farm' implies that we are making belts and wallets out of our charges. We are not, thus adding the words 'zoological park' drives home what we are really about. We are

A bird rookery on the grounds of the St. Augustine Alligator Farm Zoological Park.

Doug Alderson

accredited with the American Zoo and Aquarium Association (AZA), and do a lot more than breed alligators."

And what is the key to the success of the longest-lasting alligator attraction in Florida? "We try to never look like we are more than 125 years old," said Bruegger. "The owner of the Alligator Farm invests a lot back into the park every year, adding things like Komodo dragon exhibits, zip lines, kids play areas, etc. This keeps us relevant and interesting."

GATORAMA

Gatorama is located in Palmdale on U.S. 27, about eighteen miles south of State Road 70. Address: 10665 N. U.S. Highway 27, Palmdale, FL 33944; (863) 765-0623

In tiny Palmdale near Lake Okeechobee, Gatorama opened in 1957 and still thrives. The attraction features a one-thousand-foot boardwalk to enable visitors to view thousands of alligators and crocodiles along with a pair of Florida panthers, bobcats, skunks, raccoons, and exotic animals such as peacocks, African tortoises, macaws, and kinkajous (a South American mammal related to raccoons). Every August, Gatorama features an alligator hatching festival in which visitors can witness the hatching of thousands of baby alligators emerging from their shells, chirping loudly for their mothers. There is an extra charge for visitors to hold an

Florida Tourists.

Photo copyright 1907. The Hugh C. Leighton Co.

Published by Hugh C. Leighton Company of Portland, Maine, and printed in Germany

Humorous 1907 photo of alligators driving two women in a Model A.

egg so they can experience an alligator hatching in their hands—one of the innovative bonus offerings that have enabled the attraction to survive.

"Gatorama continues to thrive because we are flexible," said co-owner Patty Register. "We change as the guests' desires and expectations for entertainment change. We try to be true to our identity and never forget that guests want truth and sizzle. We are sometimes seeing four generations of the same families coming back to Gatorama. Alligators have an undeniable mystery about them. We think families love doing business with other families and appreciate that we are the genuine article!

Fifth-generation Florida Crackers! We are fortunate indeed."

The beauty of attractions such as Gatorama is that, being more compact, they do not have the great overheads of more massive attractions of the past. And they seem more immune to trends, since non-southerners never appear to tire of seeing large, potentially man-eating crocodilians from a safe perch.

Both the small and the large roadside attractions throughout the state prove that as long as there are tourists, the alligator will remain a prime symbol of Florida. In turn, the Florida tourism industry owes a debt of gratitude to the American alligator.

EIGHT

Bok's Tower Still Sings

◇◇◇◇◇◇◇◇◇◇◇◇◇◇◇◇

"Created to provide a retreat of natural beauty for the human, a refuge for birds, a study of Southern planting and a harmonious setting for the Singing Tower. . . . Such a Sanctuary is a place set apart from the unrest of modern life, and where in Nature's healing beauty and in a conducive calm, man can find that inspiration which is as necessary to civic or domestic life as it is to art."

Major H. M. Nornabell, *sanctuary director (1929)*

To find Bok Tower Gardens, take the scenic highway (U.S. 27A and State Road 17) to Lake Wales. Just north of town, head east 2.6 miles on Burns Avenue to the attraction. Address: 1151 Tower Blvd., Lake Wales, FL 33853; (863) 676-1408

Standing like a mythic pinnacle atop Iron Mountain near Lake Wales, Bok Tower—or Singing Tower, as it was once called—is the culmination of a multiyear vision of Edward Bok in the 1920s, and it has been singing since it opened in 1929. "Singing" refers to the sixty carillon bells that were hoisted upward through the center of the neo-Gothic/art deco–style tower during its creation and now expertly played by carillonneur Geert D'hollander of Belgium. He is only the fourth carillonneur to be stationed at the tower in its long history. "My Dad was a carillonneur in Belgium and when I was seventeen [1982], we flew here to Lake Wales because he wanted me to see one of the best carillon towers in the world," he said from his spacious office on the sixth floor of the bell tower. "I fell in love with the place."

The largest bell weighs nearly twelve tons and is played with a foot pedal. When struck with the metal clapper inside the bell, attached to the keyboard with wires, it can vibrate for more than two minutes. The other bells—the smallest weighing sixteen pounds—are played by foot pedals and by hitting paddle-like knobs on the keyboard with closed hands. The range of sounds covers nearly five octaves. "The bells never have to be retuned," explained my guide, then marketing manager Brian Ososky, "but most carillon bells have to be replaced after 250 to 300 years, so that is a

Historic Bok Tower today.

Doug Alderson

problem future managers will have to grapple with."

What sets Bok Tower apart from other bell towers is its location. Most carillon bells throughout the world are in big cities and on busy college campuses. "When you stop playing, you hear the traffic," said D'hollander. But at Bok Tower, the bells resonate through a quiet space with only breezes and birds as accompaniment. Visitors are asked to keep quiet when the bells are being played.

"It is nature's concert hall," added Ososky.

While D'hollander played his 3 p.m. concert with the bells, Ososky guided me through the tower's archival room and library. The library boasts the largest collection of carillon books and music in the world, while the archives hold historical photos, original blueprints, correspondence, early guest books, and other memorabilia from the tower's long history. Notebooks showcase some of the two thousand

Some of Lee Lawrie's designs on the outside of Bok Tower.

Doug Alderson

different postcards of the attraction that were produced by various companies over the decades.

At different floor levels, Ososky and I stepped out on small balconies to admire sweeping views and the tower's sculptural elements designed by Lee Lawrie. At ground level, there are twelve interpretive signs of the zodiac in a pink marble sundial. At thirty feet, carved marble pelicans, herons, fish, and scenes from *Aesop's Fables* reach toward the sky. At 130 feet, the sides are adorned with more majestic birds along with jellyfish, seahorses, and other sea creatures. Swans, foxes, storks, tortoises, hares, and baboons can be seen as well. At 150 feet, the square base changes to an octagon where four marble finials of eagles survey the scene below. Massive tile grilles by J. H. Dulles Allen depict doves carrying laurel and oak branches as symbols of strength, peace, and goodwill.

Eight marble herons fourteen feet tall grace the top of the tower, a wel-come change from the gargoyles of Gothic tradition. Reinforcing and decorating the steel frame, the primary building materials used were salmon-colored coquina rock from St. Augustine and gray and pink marble from north Georgia, making for an aesthetically pleasing combination. The entire tower is surrounded by a fifteen-foot moat filled with koi fish.

What could easily have taken a decade or more to construct took only two years under the guidance of designer and builder Milton Medary. "In a single, simple unit, [the tower] must sing of music, sculpture, color, architecture, landscape design and the arts of the workers in brass and iron, ceramics, marble and stone—each part of a chorus, each adding beauty to the others," said Medary about his work. The architectural feat has been called America's Taj Mahal.

We descended to the bottom level, what is known as the Founder's Room. This was once reserved for Bok's family

The ornate tile floor of the Founder's Room on the bottom level of Bok Tower.

Doug Alderson

Geert D'hollander of Belgium plays Bok Tower's carillon bells.

Doug Alderson

and contains original furniture and family heirlooms. A multicolored tile floor created by J. H. Dulles Allen is a mandala of animals, sea creatures, and natural elements. If Henry David Thoreau had ever wanted to build a monument to nature's beauty, the Singing Tower would be it.

As D'hollander finished his concert near the top of the tower, we approached the giant teak door to the outside, one adorned with thirty hand-crafted brass panels depicting the biblical story of creation. It was created by famous metalworker Samuel Yellin, who also designed the decorative iron gates on the north side of the tower. When we pulled it open and stepped into the light, appreciative visitors applauded, as they thought one of us was the carillonneur. "No, no, it's not us," Ososky said. "The carillonneur, Geert D'hollander, is coming out in a minute to answer any of your questions."

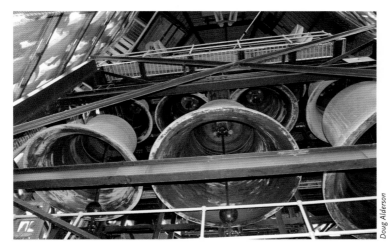

Some of the large carillon bells housed at Bok Tower.

Doug Alderson

Then he whispered to me, smiling, "I've never had that happen before." Despite the mistaken identity, it was a warm feeling.

Bok remembered carillon bells in his native Netherlands as a boy and wanted to present the tower and surrounding fifty-five-acre botanical garden as a gift to the American people to show his appreciation for the opportunities the country and people had given him. After all, he had become a successful journalist and editor of the *Ladies Home Journal*, the most popular magazine of the time. He made millions as a mover and shaker in the publishing industry.

To begin his project, Bok hired Frederick Law Olmsted Jr., son of the famous New York Central Park creator, to lay out the gardens in 1921. He directed Olmsted to transform the sand hill into "a spot of beauty second to none in the country." Trenches were dug for irrigation pipes, and thousands of loads of rich soil were brought in.

The planting began in 1923 and continued for five years. The grand total was astounding—ten thousand azaleas, one thousand live oaks, one hundred sabal palms, three hundred magnolias, and a host of other species. Special emphasis was placed on growing native and nonnative food plants for migratory birds. Paths were purposely placed without signage so that visitors could intuitively guide themselves to the highest points on the property to behold a vista—unusual for Florida—or to view the tower and reflection pool. The grounds were believed to be sacred by Native Americans, a high point used for worship. For this reason, four Seminole chiefs visited in 1930, and a group of Seminoles returned each spring for several years to set up camp and showcase their culture.

President Calvin Coolidge presided over the garden and tower's dedication in 1929, with sixty to seventy thousand people in attendance. Bok died a year

Bird's-eye view from the Bok Tower.

Doug Alderson

later, but his vision and guiding principles endure. "Make you the world a bit better and more beautiful because you have lived in it," Bok's grandmother once told him, and this principle remains part of the attraction's mission statement.

"Bok would be very happy that his idea has survived the test of time—the economy, hurricanes, and most of all, the modern culture," said foundation president David Price. "There was a big push in Florida to monetize attractions and this is something Bok did not want to do. He did not want to have politics, commercialism or theology overtake it."

While the Bok Tower image ended up on postcards, plates, salt and pepper shakers, and even a 1941 Kellogg's Rice Krispies box, the attraction's managers have sought to remain true to the site's mission of being a sanctuary. Soon after Bok's son Curtis took

over as manager in 1956, he was approached by Billy Graham to do a crusade at the attraction, but he refused. "It's a spiritual place, not a religious place," Price explained. "Edward Bok wanted to do something for world peace and to create a peaceful place where man and animals were in harmony and people could think freely. He is still as relevant today as he was then. People need a place for respite and rejuvenation."

Despite its lack of commercialism, the Bok Tower Gardens became a focal point for Florida tourism in the 1940s and 1950s, with more than six hundred thousand visitors a year. The tourism magnet helped to spawn a nearby attraction, the Great Masterpiece, a three-hundred-thousand-piece mosaic rendering of Leonardo da Vinci's *The Last Supper* that was once hidden from Nazis in a European basement. By the 1960s and 1970s, the mosaic was sur-

The Bok Tower was featured on a 1941 Rice Krispies box.

Doug Alderson

rounded by a western fort, glass blowers, gardens, a miniature golf course, animal shows, an alligator pool, a train ride, and a treetop cable car. The name was changed to Masterpiece Gardens, and it, Bok Tower, and Cypress Gardens along the popular Orange Blossom Trail, U.S. 27, came to be labeled "The Big Three" of central Florida. But Masterpiece Gardens didn't survive the Disney-inspired tourism shift to Orlando, whereas Bok Tower endured. The property is now used for retreats and church camps, and the mosaic is currently housed at Bob Jones University, a religious college in South Carolina.

Today, visitation at Bok Tower Gardens has been steadily rising. The attraction has endured tough times because Bok had the foresight to create an endowment that has grown steadily, hovering around $40 million. Only a small portion is used each year. And through a highly successful $12 million capital campaign, the current management and board recently embarked on a careful expansion to make the attraction more appealing and accessible to all age groups. The first phase included a children's garden, edible display garden, Florida wild garden and preserve, tower restoration, and more trails that are accessible to both wheelchairs and strollers.

A rising star in landscape architecture, Thomas Woltz, was hired to plan this new phase in Bok Tower Gardens' evolution. "One of the most exciting things about Bok Tower is its ability to reach people emotionally," Woltz said in the attraction's glossy newsletter, the *Garden Path*. "The idea of sanctuary, of beauty, of people immersed in nature presents a tremendous opportunity to capture their imagination and emotions. And that's a very important moment when you have someone's emotional attention because you can start to tell other stories. As people come to know more about this place, Bok Tower Gardens can help build a new generation of environmental stewards."

As part of that effort, the attraction helps to rescue rare native plants

Bok Tower Gardens marketing manager Brian Ososky (left) and foundation president David Price show off a map of the gardens and planned expansion.

Doug Alderson

impacted by development or road projects. Plants, seeds, and cuttings are brought back to the gardens to be potted and eventually reintroduced to areas undergoing restoration. The attraction is also curating a national collection of rare native plants, boasting sixty-four different species and counting. This effort serves as a buffer against extinction.

In order to ensure survivability of Bok Tower Gardens, annual events are designed for broad appeal. These range from symphonic concerts in December to dance music in the spring to holiday home tours of the historical Pinewood Estate on the property. Art and history exhibits and workshops are held throughout the year. "Some people call us the area's best kept secret," said Ososky. "Even some residents of Lake Wales don't know what that tower on the hill is, but we're trying to get the word out. We want to do more with young families. They will be the gardens' future members."

Published by Morse's Photo Service in Lake Wales and printed by the Albertype Company of Brooklyn, New York; no copyright

A Bok Tower postcard from the early 1940s.

NINE

Mixing Old and New at LEGOLAND

◇◇◇◇◇◇◇◇◇◇◇◇◇◇

LEGOLAND and Cypress Gardens are located in Winter Haven. From I-4, take Exit 55 and head south seventeen miles on U.S. 27. Turn right (west) on State Road 540/Cypress Gardens Boulevard and travel four miles to the attraction. Address: 1 Legoland Way, Winter Haven, FL 33884; (877) 350-5346

As you drive through the Orlando area, billboards announce the various theme parks—Disney World, SeaWorld, Universal Studios, the Wizarding World of Harry Potter. All are within a few miles of each other, except one—LEGOLAND Florida. To reach this theme park, launched in 2011, one has to take I-4 west from Orlando to U.S. 27 and then head south twenty-two miles to Winter Haven. That's because LEGOLAND Florida was built on the foundation of the defunct Cypress Gardens, one of Florida's classic attractions and what the new owners call the soul of the park.

LEGOLAND Florida is an interactive park with eleven distinct themed zones that's geared toward young families with children between the ages of two and twelve. There are giant Lego animals and dragons, various rides, a water park, and a plaza where replicas of famous structures and cities are built out of Legos. Many of the elements are unique to Florida theme parks, and large live oaks provide am-

No source listed

Brochure from Cypress Gardens in its earlier days.

ple shade. Other elements draw from the earlier Cypress Gardens, such as the water-skiing and stunt shows. The difference is that the water shows are

The entrance to Cypress Gardens today, with a southern belle made of Legos.

Doug Alderson

Close-up of the made-from-Legos hoop-skirted southern belle at the entrance to Cypress Gardens.

Doug Alderson

geared more toward children, with the skiers dressed like Lego characters. A Lego pirate ship is anchored near the grandstand where the pirate "Brickbeard" fights against a brave female protagonist. And the historical Magnolia Mansion looks much the same, except it is now Buddy's Character Corner, where visitors can interact and take photos with costumed Lego characters.

The twenty-two acres of the original Cypress Gardens, fully restored, is where the old Cypress Gardens resonates the strongest. There are even colorful hoop-skirted southern belles that have long been associated

View toward the historical wedding chapel at Cypress Gardens.

Doug Alderson

with the gardens, only they are now immovable life-size statues made of (what else?) Legos! From a distance, you can't tell. The detail is astounding. It's just part of the interesting juxtaposition of old and new at LEGOLAND.

Strolling through the historical attraction, one can visit the wedding pagoda on a hill overlooking Lake Eloise where countless weddings were held. Weddings are no longer allowed at LEGOLAND since they don't fit in with the attraction's targeted demographic. Most adult visitors are already married with children.

The classic Florida Pool, shaped like the Sunshine State for the 1953 movie *Easy to Love* starring Esther Williams, has been fully restored. Only, during my visit, it wasn't filled with floating oranges and grapefruit and ringed by beautiful women as in early photo shoots.

The great banyan tree, planted as a sapling by founder Dick Pope in 1939, grows ever larger, now covering a span of fifty-five feet. The gardens are lush and tropical looking, and some of the ponds and canals harbor real alligators, not just the bright green Lego alligator at the foot of the park's man-made waterfall. "We are really fortunate to have the gardens," said Audrey Padgett, LEGOLAND Florida's marketing manager. "Most theme parks end up being a concrete jungle, but we have inherited a botanical garden. It really showcases Florida and it's a great place for families to relax and slow down after they've been through other parts of the attraction."

Phil Royle, product excellence manager, added, "Our general manager [Adrian Jones] is passionate about maintaining this as the most beautiful LEGOLAND park in the world. He was

Made by Tichnor Brothers of Boston and published by Cypress Gardens Gift Shop

Vintage postcard featuring models around the Florida-shaped pool at Cypress Gardens.

The Florida Pool today.

Doug Alderson

The massive banyan tree in Cypress Gardens planted by the Popes in 1939.

Doug Alderson

told that the only way he would lose his job was if he allowed the banyan tree to die."

To keep the massive tree alive during freeze events, the attraction has replaced the old fire pits from the Cypress Gardens era with thirty-five gas outlets for space heaters. A stroll through the gardens is a walk through Florida's golden age of tourism, where millions of visitors were engrained with the image of Florida as a tropical wonderland. Besides Florida, Merlin Entertainment has several other LE-GOLAND attractions worldwide, with more being planned.

While visiting LEGOLAND Florida, let's say that you're not too keen on playing with Legos or riding roller coasters and are more interested in touring the old Cypress Gardens. There is no separation of costs, and that can make for

an expensive outing. LEGOLAND Florida is a theme park and priced accordingly. Many local residents deal with it by buying an annual pass for just over the price of a single admission. That allows for frequent strolls through the gardens all year long.

Bob Gernert is the volunteer Cypress Gardens historian at LEGO-LAND. He does occasional history talks in the gardens. He was excited to be given a nametag made of Legos that states his new title. "I've been knighted," he said with a chuckle. Now retired, Gernert was executive director of the Winter Haven Chamber of Commerce when LEGOLAND purchased the gardens. "When we visited their attraction in California, that gave us a really good comfort level that this would be a good fit," he said. "What LEGOLAND has done is nothing short

A golden Buddha sits by a pond in the Oriental Gardens section of Cypress Gardens.

Doug Alderson

of miraculous, and they are good corporate citizens in the community."

Gernert speculates that LEGO-LAND Florida's annual visitation exceeds that of the old Cypress Gardens attraction during its peak.

> They have a natural following. When I was first hired by the chamber of commerce, one of my goals was to forge a closer bond with Cypress Gardens. It was such a huge part of our history and Florida's history. Our community was inextricably tied to it. But one of our board members said it was like dancing with a dead woman because the parking lot was often dead. Now, it has an attendance pull. The Lego Movie really increased attendance, and they [LEGOLAND] are heavily involved with the Orlando market. They are convincing people that it isn't that far to drive. It's 30 minutes from the front gate of Disney.

More wistfully, Gernert added, "If the Popes were here, I think they would embrace LEGOLAND because it is family oriented and very wholesome. Cypress Gardens employees from the 1950s and '60s speak of it as being a family. Mrs. Pope was a second mother to many of the employees and she kept them in line. Their business model was to provide something for the whole family to enjoy. And if they saw that the original park was on the national register of historic places and the gardens were as nice as they are, they would be delighted."

As you leave the gardens and wander through the larger LEGOLAND village, the image of Florida as a fanta-

A vintage Cypress Gardens postcard.

An alligator made of Legos. Wild alligators live at the attraction as well.

Doug Alderson

Florida's Capitol Building re-created in Legos at LEGOLAND.

syland—not just a tropical paradise—is at the forefront. In this regard, it has more in common with most Orlando theme parks. But there is a difference. LEGOLAND rarely has the huge crowds and long lines of those other attractions, and the attraction has a smaller employment base and footprint. "This place does not have the frantic feel to it like the Orlando parks," said Audrey Padgett. Amen to that. Frantic is not how one should feel when walking the hallowed ground of Cypress Gardens.

TEN

The Many Lives of Marineland

◇◇◇◇◇◇◇◇◇◇◇◇◇◇◇◇

Marineland is located on State Road A1A about twenty miles south of St. Augustine. From I-95 South, take Exit 305 and head east on State Road 206. Upon reaching A1A, turn right and follow seven miles south to attraction. From I-95 North, take Exit 289 and head east on Palm Coast Parkway until reaching A1A. Head north eight miles. Address: 9600 Oceanshore Blvd., St. Augustine, FL 32080; (904) 471-1111 or (877) 933-3402

Perhaps no other Florida attraction has performed a Houdini act with fate like Marineland. The attraction, opened in 1938 to great fanfare along a remote strip of State Road A1A just north of Daytona Beach, has gone through several transformations, with closures and rumors of closures, only to reemerge with an altered image.

Initially called Marine Studios, it was created primarily to film underwater scenes for television and motion pictures. It was an untried endeavor, conceived by Ilya Tolstoy (grandson of Russian novelist Leo Tolstoy), producer and explorer Sherman Pratt, and two wealthy cousins, producer Cornelius Vanderbilt Whitney and producer and writer W. Douglas Burden. They worked with Jacksonville filmmaker Merian Cooper, producer of the original *King Kong*. Many doubted that a

The old entrance to the Marineland aquariums still stands.

Doug Alderson

facility could be built of adequate size to meet the needs of both large marine animals and filming. The designers proved the skeptics wrong, creating the world's first oceanarium. The oceanarium buildings had numerous portholes that enabled visitors and a growing number of marine researchers and film crews to peer into an undersea world as if from a submarine. The architecture was described as "nautical moderne." Writers with the Works Progress Administration (WPA) in 1939 described the tanks, with their square portholes, as "resembling a stranded Caribbean cruiser." The WPA guide writers added,

> Two great tanks, one round, the other rectangular, contain many varieties of deep-sea life. Through the portholes visitors see porpoises, sawfish, sharks, giant green turtles, shrimp, the manta (devilfish), and numerous common food fish. Brilliantly colored tropical fish swim in sea gardens of coral and algae, while penguins brought from Robbin Island off the African coast paddle on the surface.

When the tanks were first stocked (May 1938), experts were unable to predict which species would live amicably together. They found that porpoises, sharks and sawfish can share the same tank. A black grouper, however, recently swallowed a shark. The menhadens are not attacked because of their odor.

During World War II, the attraction closed to the public because both the staff and the facility were needed for the war effort. The Coast Guard worked on developing shark repellent at the oceanarium, and a high point on the property was used as a lookout for enemy submarines in the Atlantic. The postwar baby boom was kind to the facility when it reopened to the public in 1946, and it enjoyed several good years. The attraction boasted the first successful dolphin birth in human care

Vintage postcard showing portholes at old Marine Studios.

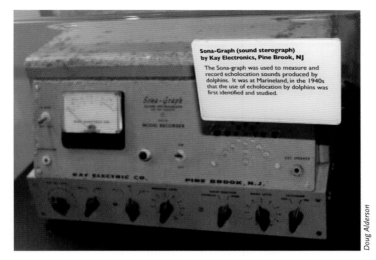

Marineland's "Sona-Graph" machine from the 1940s.

Doug Alderson

in 1947, a calf named Spray. Behind the scenes, using a sonagraph, Marineland researchers were the first to measure and record dolphin echolocation and other sounds, an effort that continues as scientists seek to break the code of dolphin communication.

Marineland also came upon something quite by accident that would help to emblazon its image in the eyes of the public. Handlers noticed that dolphins in the oceanarium seemed highly intelligent and were doing tricks and maneuvers at feeding time, perhaps seeking extra fish. When handlers held fish higher and higher, dolphins would oblige by jumping and leaping. A question was posed: Could a dolphin be trained?

In 1949, veteran circus animal trainer Adolf Frohn was hired in the first-ever attempt to train dolphins, focusing on a highly intelligent dolphin named Flippy. By 1951, Flippy had learned six behaviors as part of the world's first aerial dolphin act: ringing a suspended bell, honking a bulb horn, catching a football, raising a flag, towing a surfboard with either a small dog or a girl aboard, and bursting through a paper-covered hoop. Frohn even trained Flippy to swim onto a stretcher for medical care—another first.

Marineland also stayed true to its roots as a film studio. It helped to produce feature films, such as providing underwater footage for parts of *Creature from the Black Lagoon* in 1954 and the much-anticipated sequel, *Revenge of the Creature*, in 1955. Underwater scenes for the television series *Sea Hunt* were also filmed at Marineland, followed by a *Benji* television movie in which the four-legged canine star actually took a scuba dive with a large glass dome over his head—a first. During these glory years, the attraction often drew more than three hundred thousand visitors annually. Celebrities of the time also frequented

Vintage postcard showing feeding time at Marine Studios.

Feeding Time at Marine Studios. Marineland. Florida 54

the attraction's Moby Dick Lounge. These included Ernest Hemingway and Marjorie Kinnan Rawlings.

Given Marineland's pioneering success, copycats were inevitable. The first was the Miami Seaquarium, opened in 1955. The new rival lured away several key dolphin trainers who eventually created the world's best-known dolphin: Flipper. Marineland's Flippy had difficulty competing with a television star. Other rivals included Ocean World in Fort Lauderdale, the Aquatarium in St. Petersburg, Sea-Orama in Clearwater Beach, Neptune's Garden in Marathon, Theater of the Sea in Islamorada, and Gulfarium in Fort Walton Beach. Still, Marineland persevered and remained one of Florida's top attractions during the 1960s and into the 1970s. Because the surrounding town was called Marineland, Marine Studios changed its name to Marineland in 1961 so it would be on all the maps. And people had begun calling it Marineland anyhow. After a sister Marineland attraction was launched in Los Angeles, "Florida" was added to the name.

My family loved Marineland, with its leaping dolphins, when we visited

Marineland rack card from the 1960s.

International Graphics of Hollywood, Florida

in 1968. The favorable impression stayed with me. My wife and I took my then nine-year-old daughter there in 1994, a visit that helped spark her interest in dolphins and marine life. She minored in biology in college with an emphasis on marine biology.

The emergence of SeaWorld Orlando in 1973, a mega marine theme park, took the biggest bite out of Marineland's attendance. The historical attraction went through several owners, closed briefly in 1999 due to Hurricanes Floyd and Irene, and closed for longer in 2004 due to damage from Hurricanes Charley, Frances, and Jeanne. While planners worked on a design to create more hands-on experiences with marine mammals at the facility, several of the historical structures and exhibits had to be demolished, and some of the property was sold to the Trust for Public Land to be turned over to Flagler County for a park. Most observers believed that the world's first oceanarium would suffer the same fate as Six Gun Territory and other Florida attractions, but Marineland morphed again. A new 1.3-million-gallon facility was built that focused more on animal-human interactions and education. When the park reopened in 2006, it was known as Marineland's Dolphin Conservation Center, and in 2011 it was sold to Georgia Aquarium and renamed Marineland Dolphin Adventure. Today, guests can swim with dolphins for a half hour ("The Immersion"), touch and feed dolphins, become a trainer for a day, and enjoy other close encounters, including holding a canvas over the water and allowing a dolphin to paint a masterpiece with three primary colors. Or they can pay a more modest admission fee to simply watch dolphins.

In touring the revamped Marineland Dolphin Adventure with my guide, education and community development manager Terran McGinnis, I missed many of the old buildings that I remembered from past visits but

Marineland's Terran McGinnis poses with vintage items from the attraction's past.

Doug Alderson

enjoyed the frolicking dolphins in the more accessible pools that have been built. "It was always our intent to keep the historic buildings," said McGinnis, "but the 2004 hurricanes did enough damage that engineers deemed them unsafe and non-salvageable. It was heartbreaking."

Even though this is not the Marineland of the past, the attraction's mission is evolving and becoming more expansive. Besides the focus on dolphin interactions, Marineland is seeking to breed increasingly rare sand tiger sharks. "Our ability to pull in ocean water just as the original Marine Studios did, with seasonally fluctuating light and temperature conditions of our outdoor habitats, may provide just the right environment for these animals," said McGinnis. Marineland takes in injured sea turtles and is seeking to develop a touch tank with spotted eagle and cownose rays.

For the dolphin facility, various tanks are connected with gates and channels that allow animals to be together or divided into social groups as circum-

A dolphin mugs for the camera at Marineland.

Doug Alderson

stances may require, often changing throughout the day. Certain dolphins may be in a tank because they play well together, or breeding may be desired, or a mother dolphin is nursing an offspring. "We have a healthy social group of dolphins and breeding behavior is a sign of the health of this community," said McGinnis. "I have had the opportunity to see many babies born here over the years, usually in the middle of the night." There has been a voluntary moratorium on collecting wild bottlenose dolphins since the 1980s.

One small tank has a lift so a dolphin can be raised for examination by a veterinarian. When not being exam-ined, dolphins are frequently brought into the examination pool for play and treats so they develop a positive association with the procedure. Certain play techniques that include rubbing bellies and tails make it easier to conduct medical procedures such as ultrasounds and taking blood. "Because of preventive health care, we have dolphins living here into their forties, fifties, and sixties," said McGinnis. Nellie, a Marineland dolphin that recently passed away at age sixty-one, was the oldest known dolphin to have lived in human care.

And while Marineland is all about encouraging humans to interact with dolphins at the facility, "in the wild,

Dolphins still leap for visitors at Marineland.

the kindest thing you can do is to give them space," said McGinnis. "That is a priority for us. We don't want people generalizing their interaction with these dolphins to interacting with wild dolphins." Part of Marineland's education program revolves around the Marine Mammal Protection Act of 1972. This includes informing people that feeding dolphins in the wild is prohibited. "They begin to associate people in boats with food, and as a result, they can be struck and injured or killed by boats."

And while Marineland's dolphins, like most animals in human care, will never know the wild and the risks associated with it, McGinnis views Marineland's role as motivating people to care about dolphins and other marine life. "The core issue is protecting this planet," she said. "We fill a particular niche for those people who need direct contact with animals to find the inspiration to tread more lightly on the planet." And that's something Marineland has been doing well, under different identities, since 1938.

A trainer works with a dolphin at Marineland.

ELEVEN

Solomon's Castle in the Swamp

◇◇◇◇◇◇◇◇◇◇◇◇◇◇

Solomon's Castle is forty-five miles due east of Bradenton. From I-75, take State Road 64 and head east twenty-eight miles (or from U.S. 17 head west ten miles on State Road 64). Travel south on County Road 665 about ten miles. Look for hand-painted signs. The attraction is on the left. Address: 4533 Solomon Rd., Ona, FL 33865; (863) 494-6077 (Do not follow GPS units to the physical address, as some units will lead travelers to an orange grove three miles away!)

A man's home is his castle, the old saying goes. But what happens when a man's home *is* a castle? A shiny castle looms above Florida's tree line, and it's not Cinderella's Castle in Disney World. Solomon's Castle, designed and built by artist and sculptor Howard Solomon forty-five miles east of Bradenton, is so remote that the attraction's website recommends filling up with gas before you leave civilization: "The fun part! Finding us!" How

Solomon's Castle glistens in the midday sun thanks to hundreds of aluminum printing plates used for siding.

Doug Alderson

many theme parks boast about that? To find the castle is to tour the agricultural back roads of Hardee County and follow small hand-painted signs. The two-lane roads are narrow and curvy, though paved.

Howard Solomon began building his twelve-thousand-square-foot, three-story castle in 1972, eventually covering the outside with discarded aluminum newspaper printing plates to make it silvery and reflective. Hope for a cloudy day if you plan to take photos! The glare can be blinding. Over the years, turrets and a bell tower were also added, along with a new wing for overnight guests, who get to see "what goes on at the castle after dark."

The castle served as Solomon's living quarters and remains an exhibition gallery for hundreds of his quirky works of art. Four generations of family members live on the ninety-acre property and help to run the bed and breakfast, gift shop, and restaurant.

I interviewed Solomon just before his death in 2016 at age eighty-one. A native of Rochester, New York, he explained how he inadvertently purchased the land in a flood zone, being along Horse Creek, a major tributary of the Peace River: "The realtor saw a Yankee coming. He said that if you see lots of palmettos, it won't flood. That's not true. So, when I found out I bought a swamp, I decided to build something tall."

Solomon dug a moat and used the soil to build up his castle foundation. Inside the moat, he spent four years, using 105 pilings, to build a sixty-five-foot replica of an early Spanish galleon complete with cannon ports and cannons made from drainage pipes. A drawbridge leads to the "Boat in the Moat Restaurant," run by Howard's daughter and son-in-law, and you can even feel the structure rock a bit when you're inside, but not enough to become seasick while eating lunch. An adjoining building boasts a corner lighthouse with stained-glass depictions of famous lighthouses. The restaurant and lighthouse room can fit up to 250 people.

Solomon's wife, Peggy, claims Solomon knew twenty-two trades, ranging from carpentry to welding to stained-glass work. He was kicked out of two schools for being the "class

The Boat in the Moat Restaurant.

Doug Alderson

Howard Solomon inside his castle.

Doug Alderson

clown," so nearly all of his skills were self-taught. He did his first wood carving at age four after his parents gave him a razor blade and sandpaper. It is of a truck pulling a trailer. He did his first wood inlay boxes at age nine. After a stint in the military, he worked the construction and boatbuilding trades in the St. Petersburg area before moving to the Bahamas in the 1960s to pursue metal and wood sculpture. He owned art galleries in the Bahamas and Miami before finding a chunk of "affordable swamp land" in remote Hardee County. At first, he lived in a mobile home while trying to decide what type of structure to build, but then the rainy season began. Besides wanting something tall, he needed something large enough to house his sculptures, so the castle idea was born. "It's cheaper than a

palace," he said. One day, while reading the newspaper, he saw an advertisement for used aluminum printing plates—"good for patching a roof or a chicken coop." The shiny plates proved to be watertight and durable.

When the castle was nearly finished, the local newspaper published an aerial photo of it with the headline "Hardee County's Answer to Buckingham Palace." Solomon was invited to speak to the local Kiwanis Club, where he was encouraged to open the castle to the public. He did so on the last Sunday of each month. "We started dropping brochures off at mobile home parks," Solomon explained. "That first year, we had 4,000 visitors. The next year, 8,000." Visitation and publicity steadily grew, and in 1984 the castle started opening every day except Monday. "Now, we just tell people that we have under one million visitors a year," Solomon said with a smile.

You would think that someone who could build a castle and other massive structures almost single-handedly would have the look of a body builder, but Solomon was always small and wiry. And with his gray beard, captain's hat, and playful blue eyes, he had the look of someone guiding a sailboat on open water.

After a visit to Texas, Solomon began building a replica of the famous Alamo in 2007, which he named the "Alashmo" so as not to plagiarize. It is guarded by a replica Civil War cannon with a stack of bowling balls alongside for ammunition. More of his artwork is featured in the building, and just inside the front entrance of the Alashmo is the throne room. Two throne-like chairs face each other about forty feet apart. "When my wife and I die, we're going to be stuffed and sit in those chairs and stare at each other for eternity," he said with a grin. I was getting used to that smile.

Another of Solomon's passions was antique automobiles, all Fords. Most are from the 1920s, but the oldest is a 1915 roadster. "In 2007, I watched my investments in the stock market begin to disappear," he said. "So, I took out all of my money and started buying cars. I call it my Ford 0 1 K." The antique automobile warehouse (which includes creative works by Solomon, such as sculptures of airplanes hanging from the ceiling) can also be toured by the public.

Nearly every castle window is a stained-glass design created by Solomon, and every castle section has a theme, ranging from nursery rhymes to the solar system. One clear window in his house he called his "picture window" because the sill is covered with old cameras. To view his art, and to be in his presence, is to realize that Solomon was the king of puns. He loved playing with words. For example, several "pop art" creations were made of pop-tops. A large mounted tortoise shell with hair coming out the bottom

Solomon's sculpture of a lion with a "lion's club."

THE BAND BROKE UP

Doug Alderson

Most of Howard Solomon's artwork has a humorous quality with an ample use of puns.

is called "the tortoise and the hair." A flying lawnmower sculpture is "good for mowing tall grass," and a sculpture of a woman is called "the light-headed woman" because a light bulb glows from inside her head. A child's baseball bat lies beneath a giant sculpture of a lion—"the lion's club"—and a heavy metal boat sculpture "moves real fast . . . if you want to go down." His WMD is a giant mousetrap: "Weapon of MOUSE Destruction."

There is also Solomon's gun collection: a handgun made from a toilet valve for "flushing out the perpetrator," a four-barreled pistol for Jesse James and his gang, a gun that shoots small toilet plungers known as "Plumber's Revenge," dueling pistols "made for Jack Kevorkian" with the barrels curved backward, and many more.

"We eat a lot of corn here," Peggy explained. "Corny, corny, corny." The

castle houses more than five hundred of Howard's creations, so it's a lot to take in. Solomon also enjoyed making portraits of famous people along with humorous renditions of famous artworks. A favorite is chess champion Bobby Fischer depicted in a metal sculpture of a knight chess piece.

The art pieces were largely created with discarded and recycled junk that Solomon found or that people brought to him—metal oil drums, beer cans, coat hangers, lamps, tools, appliances, bicycles, lawn mowers, brake shoes, pipes, railroad spikes, scrap lumber, and a host of other objects. They are stored in a 20-by-80-foot shed on the property, so Solomon didn't have far to walk to find inspiration.

Solomon's reward for building the castle and displaying his quirky folk art? "People take away a happy memory," he said. "They feel they have a right of discovery and they bring their friends back. We have a big percentage of repeat business." During the peak season in February and March, the castle employs six tour guides to keep up with the demand. Tours occur every fifteen minutes, and there is often a long wait. "We don't advertise at all during that time," said Solomon. "We don't want to raise the numbers of visitors." The castle is closed on Mondays and during the months of August and September when the weather is hot and buggy and "Florida is nearly empty." The Solomons use that time for upkeep and to visit friends and family.

Solomon's work is featured in galleries throughout the world, and Ripley's purchased several of his works to feature in its museums, such as a full-size horse made from coat hangers. He owned galleries in the Bahamas and the United States, and one of his proudest sculptures is of a fourteen-foot-tall polar bear eating an ice-cream cone for Borden Dairy in the Bahamas.

Solomon's creation is more than a castle in a remote swamp that people can visit. It is a testament to the fact that as long as people like Howard Solomon manifest their dreams, Florida will never be short of quirky attractions to entertain and enlighten visitors.

Doug Alderson

Howard Solomon beside his self-portrait.

TWELVE
Gardens and More Gardens

◇◇◇◇◇◇◇◇◇◇◇◇◇◇◇◇

With Florida's long growing season and reputation as a tropical paradise, garden attractions continue to flourish throughout the Sunshine State, even though only extreme southern Florida and the keys are categorized as having a true tropical climate. A few of the classic garden attractions are included in this chapter.

SUNKEN GARDENS

From I-275 in St. Petersburg, take the 22nd Avenue North exit (Exit 24) and head east. Travel 12 blocks (about a third of a mile), and turn right onto Fourth Street North. Look for the attraction on left after two blocks. Address: 1825 Fourth Street N., St. Petersburg, FL 33704; (727) 551-3102

St. Petersburg plumber George Turner bought a sinkhole and pond in 1903. He drained the water and used the fertile pond soil to grow bananas, vegetables, and flowers. He sold many of the fruits and vegetables by the roadside, and by 1926 Turner had quit the plumbing business to devote all of his time to growing fruits and vegetables and beautifying the garden. He added a series of flowing waterscapes and planted more than three hundred gardenias, eight hundred rosebushes, seven hundred azalea plants, and nearly thirty species of palms. People began stopping on Sunday afternoons to buy papayas and fruit juices and to tour the gardens. Buoyed by feedback, Turner eventually fenced off the property and officially opened Sunken Gar-

dens to the public in 1935. The initial entrance fee was fifteen cents. Eventually, concrete grottoes and cages housed tropical birds, flamingoes, tortoises, alligators, and monkeys.

The height of Sunken Gardens' popularity was in the 1960s, when yearly visitation reached three hundred thousand. Billboards advertising the gardens stretched from North Carolina to Miami. With everything going so well, the Turners purchased the adjacent Coca-Cola plant in 1967 and established the "Largest Gift Shop in the World." They created a new cave-like entrance to the gardens, and, in keeping with the unusual juxtaposition common to many Florida attractions, they added wax figurines of the life of Christ in what was known as the

An early brochure for Sunken Gardens.

"King of Kings" exhibit. The attraction's fame was also buoyed by almost five hundred professional models who used the gardens as backdrops for posed photographs. The images graced pages of newspapers nationwide, and Sunken Gardens was riding high in the sea of Florida tourism. Then along came Disney World, and the city of St. Petersburg began losing its lofty position among the tourism elite. The Turners put the garden up for sale in 1989. Ten years later, worried they might lose a cherished icon, the citizens of St. Petersburg approved a onetime tax to purchase the garden for $3.8 million. Sunken Gardens reopened to the public with great fanfare on January 5, 2000. The World's Largest Gift Shop became offices, rental space, the Great Explorations Children's Hands-On Museum, a restaurant, and a European bakery.

Visiting Sunken Gardens today involves following a maze of trails through tropical foliage with palms, live

The entrance to Sunken Gardens as it looks today.

oaks, and vine-covered arbors forming overhead canopies. The air is filled with the sweet aromas of flowering plants. A series of cascading waterfalls provides music, and in places colorful parrots greet you with a tinny "hello." Not that much has changed since Sunken Gardens opened to the public in 1935.

And while attendance at the gardens is less than what was enjoyed in its prime, the numbers are rising each year, and the attraction returns some of its annual subsidy back to the city of St. Petersburg. Several weddings a week are usually held at the gardens. Annual events include an orchid festival, the Red and Green Holiday event for the local gay and lesbian community, and Zootastic, a collaboration with the children's hands-on museum and the Lowry Park Zoo in Tampa. There are also Saturday horticulture lectures and a monthly "Family Day in the Garden."

"Visitation is rising because we have a master plan and continue to restore the gardens to their former beauty and to add enhancements,"
said Susan Rebillot, garden specialist at the attraction. "Locally, Sunken Gardens is much loved. In addition, St. Petersburg continues to be a winter home for many and has become a popular destination for visitors because of our beautiful and vibrant city. The feedback that we receive from visitors who have known the gardens for a long time is amazement and positive comments about how beautifully the gardens have been restored and maintained."

Today's Sunken Gardens boasts nearly one hundred varieties of crotons, native to the Molucca Islands of Indonesia, as well as nearly every variety of palm tree, a tropical fruit garden, a cactus and succulent garden, and a Japanese garden dedicated to St. Petersburg's sister city of Takamatsu, Japan. The original garden pathways have been restored along with a lush assortment of camellias, azaleas, water lilies, and other plants in an effort to feature a botanical garden with collections of subtropical plants rather than animal shows. Adopted parrots

A Sunken Gardens footbridge.

Doug Alderson

A winding path through Sunken Gardens.

and other birds are still displayed in aviaries, however, along with a revived flock of flamingoes. Water is recirculated through the waterscapes, and three new water features have been added. Larger aviaries are planned along with a children's garden and a garden history museum.

New employees at the gardens are put through a time-honored initiation of sorts. They sit on the "Growing Stone," a large fossilized limestone rock that was originally found by Turner in the center of the sinkhole lake. A sign describes the stone's legend: "He who sits upon the ancient stone shall be granted tranquility, inner harmony, and the talent to make things grow."

"I and many visitors pause to sit on the stone often," said Rebillot.

Judging by the lushness and variety on display at Sunken Gardens, it appears to be working.

The "Growing Stone" at Sunken Gardens was originally at the center of the sinkhole lake.

SARASOTA JUNGLE GARDENS

From I-75, take University Parkway West (Exit 213) toward Sarasota. Turn left on U.S. 41 (Tamiami Trail) and head south for two miles. Turn right on Myrtle Street and head west for three blocks. Turn right on Bay Shore Road. The entrance will be on your left. Address: 3701 Bay Shore Rd., Sarasota, FL 34234; (941) 355-1112, (941) 355-5305, or (877) 681-6547

An hour south of St. Petersburg, Sarasota Jungle Gardens was begun in the early 1930s by local newspaperman David Breed Lindsay. Lindsay was fortunate to have a friend and neighbor in Pearson Conrad, who owned an adjacent nursery. The two teamed up to landscape the ten-acre site. As with most Florida garden attractions, exotic plants and trees—including the rare Australian nut tree—were brought in from throughout the world and interspersed with native trees such as bald cypresses, red maples, oaks, and royal palms. Soon after the attraction was purchased by Arthur Allyn in 1971, parrots and cockatoos (trained by California prisoners to talk and do tricks) became a top attraction. The popular show was aptly named "The Jail Birds."

Sarasota Jungle Gardens still flourishes. Partly because of its longevity, the garden now boasts the largest Norfolk Island pine in Florida, and the classic bird shows continue. The attraction is family operated by the descendants of Arthur Allyn.

Also in Sarasota is the fifteen-acre Marie Selby Botanical Garden, once a private estate of the Selby family and opened to the public in 1975. The garden specializes in epiphytic plants, making it unique among most formal gardens in Florida and elsewhere.

No source listed

A vintage brochure for Sarasota Jungle Gardens. Dating back to the 1930s, this attraction is one of Florida's survivors.

MACLAY GARDENS

The state park is located a half mile north of I-10 on U.S. 319/ Thomasville Road. Turn west on Maclay Road and immediately move into the right lane. The park entrance is a short distance on the right. Address: 3540 Thomasville Rd., Tallahassee, FL 32309; (850) 487-4556

In North Florida, Killearn Gardens was opened to the public in 1946, perched on the canopied shores of Lake Hall in the once-remote northern reaches of Tallahassee. A 1940s brochure summary of the gardens holds true today: "Here at the plantation home of the late Alfred B. Maclay one sees the original 'Aunt Jetty' Camellia and the stately and rare Italian cypress. The azalea and camellia predominate in these magnificent gardens which cover 35 acres."

Killearn Gardens was donated to the state in 1953, and the name was changed to Alfred B. Maclay Gardens State Park in the 1970s. The park today covers nearly 1,200 acres on the shores of Lake Hall, and the gardens are well maintained and certainly just as spectacular as in the days of private ownership during the peak blooming season of January through April. The original "Aunt Jetty" camellia and Italian cypresses are no more, but their clones live on in the park.

Maclay Gardens today, in spring.

RAVINE GARDENS

Follow Highway 20 (Crill Avenue) west from downtown Palatka about a mile and follow signs to Ravine Gardens State Park. Address: 1600 Twigg St., Palatka, FL 32177; (386) 329-3721

Vintage postcard showing Ravine Gardens from around 1945.

Palatka was once a bustling port city and major stop for the steamboat tourist trade. But its golden age of tourism came to a close in the early 1900s, and a subsequent freeze greatly damaged its citrus industry. The Great Depression had devastating effects on the area's already reeling economy. Thomas Byrd Gillespie, a local paving contractor, came up with idea of creating an elaborate garden to revitalize the town's tourist trade. In 1933, he paid a landscape architect to draw up a plan and then successfully lobbied city officials to embrace it. Federal funds and relief workers were obtained, and work began on the gardens, buildings, fountains, suspension bridges, a sprinkler system, terraces, and roads. The town managed Ravine Gardens until it could no longer afford to do so, so it was deeded to the state in 1970, whereupon it became a Florida state park. The gardens are best known for their thousands of blooming azaleas every spring.

WASHINGTON OAKS GARDENS

This state park is divided by State Road A1A just north of Palm Coast along Florida's east coast. The gardens can be accessed on the west side of the road, while the beach is on the east side. Address: 6400 N. Oceanshore Blvd., Palm Coast, FL 32137; (386) 446-6780

Like many of Florida's public gardens, Washington Oaks Gardens originally started as part of a private winter estate. Industrialist Owen D. Young and his wife, Louise, purchased the land in 1936 and combined native and exotic plantings and various water elements. They had both spent time in Asia, and that influence permeated the design. A few years after Mr. Young died, Mrs. Young donated the land to the state of Florida in 1965, and it became a Florida state park.

A highlight of the gardens is the Washington oak, estimated to be two to three hundred years old. It stands majestically in the center of the gardens. Visitors can also wander through the Youngs' winter estate and visit a portion of the park along the Atlantic Ocean, famous for its coquina rock shoreline.

Doug Alderson

Contemporary view of Washington Oaks Gardens State Park.

HARRY P. LEU GARDENS

From downtown Orlando, take I-4 east to Exit 85, Princeton Street. Turn right and follow the signs to Leu Gardens. Open daily from 9 a.m. to 5 p.m. Address: 1920 N. Forest Ave., Orlando, FL 32803; (407) 246-2620

Harry P. Leu and his wife, Mary Jane, purchased the Leu House and forty acres in 1936 and began establishing elaborate gardens with plants from their world travels. In 1961, the Leus donated the garden and historical home to the city of Orlando, and now it is an oasis in a rapidly growing area. A few more acres have been added to the gardens, and visitors can wander on shaded trails beneath massive oaks and past extensive camellia forests, one of the largest camellia collections in the Southeast. Like many of Florida's other garden attractions, it is a favorite place for weddings, receptions, and art exhibits.

McKEE BOTANICAL GARDEN
(formerly McKee Jungle Gardens)

The garden is located on the east side of U.S. 1 in Vero Beach at the intersection of Indian River Road. Address: 350 U.S. 1, Vero Beach, FL 32962; (772) 794-0601

During Florida's garden attraction boom, the state's east coast was not left out of the mix. In Vero Beach, Arthur McKee sought to expand his orange groves with the purchase of an eighty-acre hammock. But something about the lush vegetation and thick canopy gave him an idea. He hired designer William Lyman Philips from Bok Tower Gardens, planted hundreds of nonnative tropical plants, and opened McKee Jungle Gardens in 1932. Fitting with the "jungle" image, and to key on the post–World War II tourism boom, McKee brought in exotic animals and posed

Early McKee Jungle Gardens brochure.

beautiful women in skimpy outfits. To top it off, giant concrete mushrooms were strategically placed around the gardens.

Much of McKee Botanical Garden in Vero Beach was lost in 1976 when it was sold to a developer, but concerned citizens banded together to save at least part of it. They purchased the surviving eighteen acres for $2.1 million and eventually reopened it as McKee Botanical Garden, though keeping the original giant concrete mushrooms.

FAIRCHILD TROPICAL BOTANIC GARDEN

If traveling south on I-95, turn on U.S. 1 and travel south to SW 42nd Avenue (LeJeune Road). Turn left on SW 42nd Avenue. Travel to the roundabout and take the second right onto Old Cutler Road. The gardens are two miles on the left. Open daily from 9:30 a.m. to 4:30 p.m. Address: 10901 Old Cutler Rd., Coral Gables, FL 33156; (305) 667-8953

Although Colonel Robert H. Montgomery, a retired accountant, founded the eighty-three-acre garden in 1938, he named it after his friend, David Fairchild. Fairchild was a famous plant explorer, traveling the world in search of important food and medicinal plants. Fairchild collected several plants for the garden, including a giant African baobab tree and other unique specimens. William Lyman Philips, a leading landscape designer with the Frederick Law Olmsted partnership, designed the garden. Tropical fruits, orchids, and Florida and native plants, along with endangered plants from throughout the tropics, are part of the collection.

THIRTEEN

Other Survivors

◇◇◇◇◇◇◇◇◇◇◇◇◇◇◇◇

Nearly every region of the state boasts survivors of the golden age of Florida tourism. Some are not as robust as in the past, while others have expanded with each decade, drawing in a new generation of fans and visitors. Here is a broad selection of attractions and curiosities worthy of visitation.

SPONGEORAMA

Spongeorama is located in downtown Tarpon Springs along the main docks on the Anclote River just off Alternate U.S. 19. Address: 510 Dodecanese Blvd., Tarpon Springs, FL 34689; (727) 943-2164 or (727) 365-8793

Tarpon Springs has been associated with the Greek American sponge business for more than a century, and Spongeorama has catered to curious tourists since 1968. The retail store boasts the largest collection of natural sea sponges in the world, and the business also offers a free museum and movie to orient visitors to the community's rich history. Plus, if you

Sponge diver statue along the harbor in Tarpon Springs.

Doug Alderson

have a hankering to get on the water, the Spongeorama Cruise Lines takes visitors to view manatees, dolphins, the Anclote Lighthouse, and more.

It's fascinating just to walk the sponge docks and imagine Tarpon Springs during its heyday. The sponge industry became entrenched by 1890 but grew exponentially when Greek divers with rubberized suits and helmets were brought in. Within a few years, around fifty boats and five hundred divers had made the community famous. A Sponge Exchange was created, a tourist industry blossomed, and sponging became the largest industry in Florida. Then a blight struck in the 1940s, reducing the harvests, and it took the industry several decades to rebound. Today, the docks are alive again, and weekly sponge auctions are held. The town still has a strong Greek influence, ranging from authentic foods to art to its stately Greek Orthodox church. After a visit, you'll never want to buy a synthetic sponge again!

THE RINGLING

The Ringling, a complex of several attractions, is found in the heart of Sarasota. From I-75, take Exit 213 and head west on University Parkway toward Sarasota. Pass through the intersection of U.S. 41 (North Tamiami Trail) and onto the museum entrance road, turning right into the Florida State University Center for Performing Arts parking area. Address: 5401 Bay Shore Rd., Sarasota, FL 34243; (941) 359-5700

Vintage postcard of Ringling Brothers and Barnum & Bailey Circus performers with elephant at the circus winter headquarters in Sarasota.

S-39—At the Circus, Ringling Bros. and Barnum & Bailey Winter Quarters, Sarasota, Fla.

Since The Ringling in Sarasota combines the Museum of Art, Circus Museum, the historical Asolo Theater, the Bayfront Gardens, and more, plan to spend several hours or a couple of days to really take it in. Circus entrepreneur John Ringling originally built this complex in the early twentieth century and bequeathed it to the people of Florida. There are permanent art collections housed in a grand pink palace ranging from old masters to classical antiquities, and special exhibits are brought in from throughout the world. The circus museum features artifacts from "The Greatest Show on Earth," including a human-shooting cannon, vintage posters, and parade wagons. There are also hands-on exhibits that invite visitors to squeeze into a clown car or walk the wire. Outside, a Renaissance-style garden features bronze and stone casts of famous sculptures, including Michelangelo's *David*. It's a touch of Italy in Florida!

EDISON AND FORD WINTER ESTATES

To reach the Edison and Ford Winter Estates from I-75, take Exit 158 (Tucker's Grade) and travel west. Turn south (left) on Highway 41 through North Fort Myers and turn right on Highway 867 (McGregor Boulevard). Travel about a half mile and look for the attraction's parking lot on the left. Address: 2350 McGregor Blvd., Fort Myers, FL 33901; (239) 334-7419

Inventor Thomas Edison and inventor and industrialist Henry Ford were longtime friends and colleagues who influenced the world's technological evolution. Their winter homes are scenic and relaxing retreats that boast more than twenty acres of botanical gardens; the Edison Ford Museum, featuring a collection of groundbreaking inventions; and Edison's Botanical Research Laboratory. Stately royal palms that Edison planted line the walkways and entrance road, and the grounds boast hundreds of tropical and flowering plants and champion trees. It is tropical Old Florida at its best.

SHELL FACTORY

To reach the Shell Factory from I-75, take Exit 143 at Highway 78 (Bayshore Road) and head west to Business U.S. 41. Turn north and look for signs for the Shell Factory on the left. Address: 2787 N. Tamiami Trl., North Fort Myers, FL 33903; (239) 995-2141

What began as a large shell and coral retailer in Fort Myers in 1938 has morphed into a nature park with botanical trails, live animal encounters, an ecological laboratory, an alligator slough, and more. A fun park includes trampolines, bumper boats, paddleboats, a video arcade, and playful wars with water balloons. There is also a shell museum to augment the immense shell retail facility, perhaps the largest of its kind in the world. And for the price of a movie, you can try out the new Soaring Eagle Zip Line.

EVERGLADES WONDER GARDENS

To visit the Everglades Wonder Gardens from I-75, take Exit 116, turn west on Bonita Springs Road Southeast, and travel almost two miles. Turn north onto Old 41 Road, and after about a mile, the attraction is on left. Address: 27180 Old 41 Rd., Bonita Springs, FL 34135; (239) 992-2591

The Everglades Wonder Gardens in Bonita Springs, established in 1936 by Bill and Lester Piper as a home for orphaned or injured animals such as Florida panthers, closed for the first time in 2013. But award-winning photographer John Brady came to the rescue and revitalized the 3.5-acre lush botanical garden along the Tamiami Trail. New exotic plants were added, and instead of focusing on mammals, the park features a diverse collection of birds and reptiles, many of which have been rescued by wildlife officers. Museum exhibits in the entry building highlight the gardens' rich history. The park is run by a nonprofit group, the Bonita Wonder Gardens, and the city of Bonita Beach showed its love for Old Florida by providing a low-interest loan of $3.5 million.

"The Wonder Gardens is a survivor," Brady said in a 2015 *Naples Herald* article. "Places like this shut down in the blink of an eye. Then one day they're gone and we ask ourselves, 'What happened and why didn't we do something?' I wanted to bring the old jungle back to life, but I couldn't do it alone. Now the Wonder Gardens won't be just a land remembered but a place enjoyed for generations to come."

GOOFY GOLF

Goofy Golf is easy to find. It is located in the heart of Panama City Beach on Front Beach Road across from the city pier. Address: 12206 Front Beach Rd., Panama City, FL 32407; (850) 234-6403

Entrance to Goofy Golf in Panama City Beach, founded in 1959.

Doug Alderson

Several enormous concrete statues have been preserved along Panama City Beach's Miracle Strip in the Florida Panhandle. They are part of Goofy Golf, begun in 1959 by Lee Koplin. This putt-putt golf course is unlike any other. A giant purple dinosaur looms over the parking lot. Visitors can climb inside a nearly three-story rendition of an Easter Island statue or explore a black-light cave. Or they can hit a ball through the hands of a golden Buddha or through an Egyptian sphinx. There is also a castle, a giant green octopus, a stegosaurus, a windmill, and a tyrannosaurus pulling up a monkey on a chain. For many of the holes, you must time it right so that you can hit your ball without striking a moving object. At night, the eyes of many of the giant creatures glow. It's no wonder that the attraction is called "the magic world."

One reason the Panama City Beach Goofy Golf course has survived while many others haven't is because Koplin built it across from the city pier and beach on the Gulf of Mexico, always a popular location with nary a chance for a motel or condo to ever obstruct the ocean view. The place is a throwback to another era, the course is creatively laid out, and the statues are larger than most. Plus, the attraction sells the last of its stock of vintage postcards, so get them while you can!

Easter Island–style statue at Goofy Golf.

Doug Alderson

During a 2015 visit, I asked the silver-haired attendant whether Michelle, Koplin's daughter, was around. She took over when her father passed away. "Oh, she just died," the woman answered. "But the family is very sentimental about this place and they want to keep it open. People are always so happy that we're still here!"

FOUR FREEDOMS MONUMENT

The monument is located at the junction of U.S. 90 and North Range Street in the southwest corner of Four Freedoms Park in downtown Madison, Florida, zip code 32340, just north of I-10.

How did a renowned national monument happen to land in the quaint North Florida town of Madison?

In 1941, just before the bombing of Pearl Harbor, President Franklin Roosevelt famously outlined the four freedoms that form the ideals of American policy: freedom of speech and expression, freedom of worship, freedom from want, and freedom from fear everywhere in the world. "That is no vision of a distant millennium," said Roosevelt. "It is a definite basis for a kind of world attainable in our own time and generation."

Feeling that the ideals could more easily be spread through the arts, Roosevelt commissioned sculptor Walter Russell to build a monument to the four freedoms. Russell, a renaissance man who was also a musician, author, builder, and philosopher, was heralded by the *New York Herald Tribune* as "the modern Leonardo."

The monument, consisting of four angels facing different directions, was unveiled in 1943 before sixty thousand at Madison Square Garden in New York City. Roosevelt dedicated

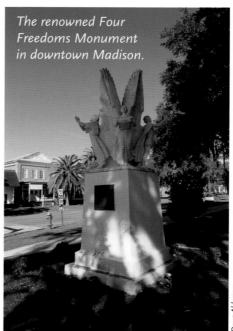

The renowned Four Freedoms Monument in downtown Madison.

Doug Alderson

the statue to Madison native Colin P. Kelly Jr., a heroic Army Air Corps captain who was killed early in World War II during a bombing mission against Japanese shipping. The monument was rededicated in Madison the following year with a speech by Florida governor Spessard Holland. Years later, other four freedoms monuments popped up in cities such as Evansville, Indiana; Cleveland, Ohio; and New York, New York.

If you visit the Four Freedoms Monument in Madison, bring your bicycle and enjoy the twelve-mile paved Four Freedoms Trail that extends into the scenic countryside from downtown.

YEARLING RESTAURANT

The Yearling Restaurant is located on Highway 325 in Cross Creek, fourteen miles southeast of Gainesville and twenty-five miles north of Ocala. Address: 14531 E. County Road 325, Hawthorne, FL 32640; (352) 466-3999

Another Old Florida relic is the Yearling Restaurant in Cross Creek, just down the road from the Marjorie Kinnan Rawlings Historic State Park and fourteen miles from Gainesville. Rawlings moved to this "half-wild, backwoods country" in 1928 and won a Pulitzer Prize eleven years later for her novel *The Yearling*. Other acclaimed books such as *Cross Creek* and *Cross Creek Cookery* followed. The restaurant first opened in 1952, closed in 1991, and reopened in 2002. It still features traditional fare from Rawlings's books—alligator tail, quail, venison, cooter (turtle), duck, frog legs, and sour orange pie—as well as more typical fare, such as chicken, flounder, catfish, clams, oysters, and prime rib. Customers debate whether it is Cracker cuisine or soul food—there is nothing "New Age"—and the period furniture and decor of the place make it a shrine to a bygone era. Blues singer Willie Greene (described as "the real deal" by slide guitarist John Hammond) frequently plays there. Take time to walk around, and bring a camera!

ANGEL'S DINER

Angel's Diner is located in downtown Palatka on Highway 17 on the south side of the highway. Open twenty-four hours a day! Address: 209 Reid St., Palatka, FL 32177; (386) 325-3927

Florida's oldest surviving diner is in the St. Johns River town of Palatka. Angel's Diner opened in 1932 and is built around an old railroad dining car. It still features some of the early menu items, such as a pusalow. Never heard of a pusalow? It is a drink made with chocolate milk, vanilla syrup, and crushed ice. Period signs decorate the walls, and the narrow metal train stairs are still present. It is said that Angel's is a must-stop for any politician running for office at both the local and the state levels.

CITRUS TOWER

You can't miss the Citrus Tower since it still towers over surrounding buildings. It stands on the east side of U.S. 27 just north of the State Road 50 intersection in Clermont. Open Monday through Saturday from 7 a.m. to 7 p.m. Address: 141 North Highway 27, Clermont, FL 34711; (352) 394-4061

Built in 1956 atop a high Clermont hill before Florida's turnpike and interstate highways diverted travelers, the Citrus Tower served for decades as a monument to the state's citrus industry. It was a must-stop for those traveling from Silver Springs to Cypress Gardens. The original vision called for a seventy-five-foot tower, but plans became more ambitious, and the final tower stood at 226 feet, or twenty-two stories. For many years, it was billed as Florida's highest observation point, boasting panoramic views of Florida's "ridge section." From the top, one can see thirty-five miles in any direction, or eight counties, and, like signs on a mountain summit, arrows point to various towns, cities, and attractions in different directions. One arrow still points to Cypress Gardens forty-five miles away, even though the attraction has morphed into LEGOLAND. The decor of Citrus Tower hasn't been

The observation area of Clermont's Citrus Tower with its vintage signs.

Doug Alderson

modernized much since it opened, and that is part of the draw. As someone wrote in a review, "The fifties are alive and well at the Citrus Tower Plaza."

The Clermont area has grown tremendously since the tower was built, and gone are many of the vast citrus groves once seen from the tower. In a brilliant public relations move, the tower's purpose has shifted; it now serves as "a beacon guiding a burgeoning new business and population base to the scenic South Lake County region," according to the attraction's website.

LION COUNTRY SAFARI

Lion Country Safari can be reached from I-95 by taking Southern Boulevard (Exit 68) and heading west 15.5 miles. The attraction is on the right. From the Florida Turnpike, take Southern Boulevard (Exit 97) and head west ten miles to the attraction on the right. Address: 2003 Lion Country Safari Rd., Loxahatchee, FL 33470; (561) 793-1084

In Southeast Florida, lions still roar, parrots squawk, and monkeys screech at Lion Country Safari, Parrot Jungle, and Monkey Jungle, respectively. In fact, these attractions have expanded.

Palm Beach's Lion Country Safari, opened in 1967, was billed as the world's first "cageless zoo," where visitors could drive their vehicles four miles through a large enclosure while lions, giraffes, and other animals roamed freely about. (Understandably, visitors were forbidden to step out of their vehicles for a closer look.) The idea, conceived and developed by a group of South African and British entrepreneurs, was to bring the experience of an African game park to the American public.

Lion Country Safari now boasts more than nine hundred animals, including lions, white rhinos, chimpan-zees, zebras, and giraffes. They can be viewed in the drive-through preserve and in the improved Safari World exhibit area. "Hundreds of thousands of people visit Lion Country Safari every year to experience the thrill of eyeball-to-eyeball viewing of magnificent animals in a natural open environment," states the website. There are also nine carnival rides and a water "sprayground," where the idea is to cool off from the Serengeti . . . er, I mean, South Florida heat.

"When we first opened in 1967 we were primarily just a lion park," said Esther Sierra-Valentin, marketing coordinator for the attraction. "We have added about a hundred different species now, added a walk-through park and a KOA [Kampgrounds of America] campground. The south Florida climate has been ideal for our animals and business. We add new species and attractions as we can. This helps us to stay relevant. We try to add something new in the walk-through park every couple of years."

According to Sierra-Valentin, one key to Lion Country Safari's success (and that of many others) is cross promotion with attractions throughout the state.

JUNGLE ISLAND (formerly Parrot Jungle)

To reach Jungle Island from I-95, take I-395 East (MacArthur Causeway), Exit 2D. Cross over the bridge and take the first right after the bridge onto Parrot Jungle Trail. Follow the road around and under the bridge to the parking garage on the left side. Address: 1111 Parrot Jungle Trl., Miami, FL 33132; (305) 400-7000

South Miami's Parrot Jungle opened in 1933, occupying the site of a former nudist colony. Most of the tropical birds were not caged but rarely ventured far from their food source. Several years ago, on a visit with my wife and daughter, a large blue parrot nipped my daughter's finger, and I was amazed at how many employees quickly emerged from the tropical foliage upon hearing her screams. No one seemed surprised, and my daughter was unhurt—only pinched a bit.

Parrot Jungle morphed into Jungle Island in 2007 after a move to Watson Island. While exotic birds are still a main feature, the attraction has expanded to include big cats, primates, giant tortoises, kangaroos, and even South African penguins. A private beach and a floating aqua park along Biscayne Bay are also featured.

MONKEY JUNGLE

To reach Monkey Jungle from the north or west, follow Florida Turnpike Extension South to Exit 11 (SW 216 Street) (also labeled for Cutler Ridge Boulevard). Upon exiting, go to the bottom of the ramp, and then continue through the first intersection. Turn right onto SW 216th Street and drive four miles west. Monkey Jungle will be on your right-hand side. Address: 14805 SW 216th St., Miami, FL 33170; (305) 235-1611

Monkey Jungle, just south of Miami, is an attraction where "the humans are caged, and the monkeys run wild." Visitors walk in caged corridors while the monkeys live in their "natural state," climbing around in a large enclosure. An early brochure describes the attraction's evolution: "Early in

1933 a small group of monkeys were imported from Singapore and liberated to this natural jungle more or less as an experiment. Not only did this little band of immigrants from far off Asia find the jungle satisfactory, but they set up their own society ruled by a chief and took over 'their' jungle so completely that it was soon found necessary to construct a caged walkway to protect visitors from the jealous monkey inhabitants." Other types of monkeys were added, such as those from the Amazon rain forest, along with beloved chimpanzees.

The primate population at Monkey Jungle has expanded over the years, as primates are apt to do when left to roam in a protected preserve. Of the more than three hundred primates that are featured, the most popular continues to be the Java monkey troop, now numbering more than ninety individuals from an initial group of six. These monkeys are skilled divers in the wild, and they demonstrate these skills in the Wild Monkey Swimming Pool when they search for fruit thrown by the guides. Other popular spots are the Cameroon Gorilla Forest, an orangutan area, and the Amazonian Rainforest, which features three types of free-roaming monkeys: squirrel monkeys, black-capped capuchins, and howler monkeys. Most of the tropical rain forest plants in this seminatural environment came from within a hundred-mile radius of Iquitos, Peru. Monkey Jungle is now in its third generation of family ownership.

VENETIAN POOL

The Venetian Pool — Coral Gables, Florida 87

Published by Eli Witt Cigar and Tobacco Company of Miami and distributed by Tichnor Brothers of Boston

Venetian Pool postcard, circa 1945.

From U.S. 1 in Coral Gables, turn west on Bird Avenue and travel about two miles. Turn right onto Granada Boulevard and travel 0.7 miles. At the traffic circle, take the second exit onto De Soto Boulevard, and the destination will be on the right. Closed from December through February. Hours vary depending on the season. Address: 2701 De Soto Blvd., Coral Gables, FL 33134; (305) 460-5306

Created in 1923 from a coral rock quarry, the Venetian Pool is perhaps the most unique man-made aquatic facility in the country. Complete with cave-like grottoes and two waterfalls, and accentuated by palm trees, loggias, porticos, and a scenic bridge, the 820,000-gallon pool is filled and drained daily in the spring and summer and is enjoyed by both residents and visitors from around the world. When not swimming, visitors can climb two historical lookout towers for a sweeping view of Coral Gables, "The City Beautiful."

FOURTEEN
Florida Oddities Ever Popular

◇◇◇◇◇◇◇◇◇◇◇◇◇◇◇◇

Is the "golden age" of Florida tourism over? Could someone with creativity and an entrepreneurial spirit make a go of keeping a small Old Florida roadside attraction alive and thriving? How about creating a new roadside attraction? The evidence suggests that many attractions are viable as long as the elements of traffic, marketing, and innovation are present.

TARPON FEEDING AT ROBBIE'S OF ISLAMORADA

To reach Robbie's, travel about a mile south of Islamorada on the Overseas Highway/U.S. 1. Look for a sign for Robbie's on the right (bay side) just over the Lignumvitae Channel Bridge at Mile Marker 77.5. Address: 77522 Overseas Hwy., Islamorada, FL 33036; (305) 664-8070 or (877) 664-8498

In the Florida Keys, there is only one highway to reach Key West, and it's not an interstate. U.S. 1 through the keys, with its unique mile-marker system, gives many locally owned motels, restaurants, and tourist attractions an exceptional opportunity, especially since this route is highly popular with tourists, primarily during the winter months. While much of the population in northern states is hunkered down under layers of snow, visitors to the Florida Keys often enjoy tropical weather.

There are many places to stop and see on the way to Key West, and one spot, in Islamorada, is Robbie's Tarpon Feeding. You wouldn't think that a place that feeds fish would be all that popular, but tarpon aren't just any fish. They can reach more than six feet in length and live up to fifty-five years.

The tarpon-feeding attraction got its start with the goodwill of owners Robbie Reckwerdt and his wife, Mona, in 1976. They found a tarpon foundering in the shallows. When Robbie lifted the fish, he saw that the right side of its jaw had been torn open by a fisherman's gaff. He placed it in a shrimp tank and called a doctor, who showed up with his wife's mattress needles and some twine. Scarface (as the large tarpon came to be known) slowly recovered and was released into the waters off the dock six months later. He began

The dock at Robbie's on Islamorada.

Doug Alderson

to frequent the docks and sometimes brought a friend or three. Soon, more tarpon began to appear, and eventually some offspring, I am sure . . . and a tourist attraction was born!

One attractive thing about Robbie's is that it is cheap entertainment. It costs you a couple of bucks to access the dock and a few more for a bucket of fish. For this, you get to see massive tarpon sometimes breach out of the water to grab a fish before resident brown pelicans or crevalle jacks beat them to it. The tarpon have been known to grab hands holding fish dangling off the dock, but since they only have sandpaper-like teeth, they merely startle people. However, pieces of jewelry such as bracelets, watches, and rings have been lost in the process.

Tarpon looking for a meal at Robbie's.

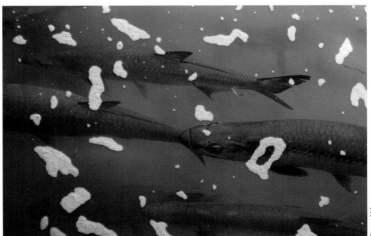

Doug Alderson

The pelicans and jacks can be a different story. Jacks have teeth, and one woman backed off the dock and into the water when she was frightened by approaching pelicans.

The tarpon feeding has spawned numerous sidewalk vendors featuring keys art, souvenirs, and food. Plus, Robbie's has a thriving restaurant and bar, along with guided sport-fishing excursions. One tourist wrote on Robbie's website:

> Robbie's is a great little place to stop. Whether you spend an hour or an afternoon here, it's great time for visitors of all ages! . . . The tarpon are huge & just swim around waiting for food. They jump out of the water for the fish & will even eat it right out of your hand if you allow them to get that close! This was also my first time getting up close to pelicans and while you are warned they can be aggressive at times, we didn't have a problem with that. Luckily for us, the docks were pretty empty, but I can see how it might not be as fun of an experience if it was crowded. There's also a cute little restaurant/bar but we didn't eat there. However, you can buy bottled beer right at the entrance to the dock so we both had a beverage while feeding the tarpon which was an added treat! We also loved walking through all the little outside shops & picked up a few souvenirs as well.
>
> We ended our day there sitting in Adirondack chairs on the little beach and watching others feed the tarpon, while herons came walking by as the pelicans flew overhead. It was picture perfect! So much so that we returned the next day. Thanks Robbie's for a great experience!

Another visitor wrote, "No matter how much you think you can hold the fish over the dock/water until they snatch it, you still jerk your hand back when they leap from the water towards your hand/fish."

On a busy day, a thousand people might visit the docks at Robbie's; many will buy fish for the tarpon, and some will eat in the restaurant and maybe buy a souvenir or two. Who says kindness doesn't pay?

Like many Old Florida–style tourist attractions, Robbie's is a melding of nature and people, a meeting ground. In this case, the fish seem tame and protected as they congregate around the docks, but they are free to come and go (and often do). Away from the docks, the tarpon are fair game as sport fish, where anglers have a thrill catching one and then releasing it. (Tarpon are not considered food fish.) Some of the fish at Robbie's have hooks in their jaws, and observers have seen them rust away over days and weeks.

BOYETT'S CITRUS ATTRACTION

From I-75, take the U.S. 98 exit to Brooksville and travel east about five miles to the stoplight at Spring Lake Highway. Turn left and go up a steep hill, and the attraction is on the right. Open Monday through Sunday from 10 a.m. to 5 p.m. Address: 4355 Spring Lake Hwy., Brooksville, FL 34601; (352) 796-2289

With reviews such as "odd funky place with Old Florida feel" and "one of Florida's best-kept secrets," Boyett's Citrus Attraction in Brooksville just might pique your interest. There is a makeshift mine for panning gold, a mini golf course, a wildlife park with a wide range of animals, and an animated pterodactyl. Oh, and there are various types of citrus, vintage arcade games, hand-dipped ice cream, and funky stuff for sale in the "Huge Florida Tourist Trap Gift Shop." Boyett's website only covers part of what is offered.

The attraction started in 1966 as an open-air citrus market for the Boyett family citrus grove, but it quickly took on elements of old-time roadside attractions that once dotted the Florida roadscapes. "You can only do so much with making oranges exciting," said co-owner Kathy Oleson, a Boyett daughter who manages the attraction with her husband, Jim. "And there was a se-

Cheyenne Alderson wearing 3-D glasses in the James Oleson art gallery at Boyett's Citrus Attraction.

Illuminated dinosaur cave at Boyett's Citrus Attraction.

Doug Alderson

vere freeze in the 1960s that destroyed much of the grove, so people started donating animals to us because we had acreage, and it just evolved from there. With all the problems we've had with growing oranges and grapefruit in the last few years, such as citrus greening, I'm glad we diversified."

On my visit, Kathy first handed out 3-D glasses to me and my family for the brightly painted wacky art gallery featuring works by her son James. Then she led us through a backdoor entrance to the heart of the attraction. "Now, there are four doors and four loops, so make sure you go through all four doors," she said.

There are lots of twists, turns, passages, and doors, but fortunately the four main doors are marked because the attraction is a fun maze to figure out. At one point you are in a cave with animated dinosaurs illuminated by black lights, something very young children might find a bit frightening if they don't know the difference between make-believe and real life. Other loops feature larger-than-life pirates, aquariums, a massive stuffed great white shark, an Old West gold mine and statues of gunslingers, animal skulls and mounts, mermaid statues, a skunk ape, a moonshine still, 1920s-era roadsters, and a vintage citrus-packing area that is still used. Mixed in are videos running on loops and displays of Old Florida souvenirs from bygone attractions. And that is all before you get to outdoor pens of live animals such as zebras, ostriches, monkeys, parrots, and llamas, some of which you can hand-feed. About the only things lacking are train rides, glass-bottom boat tours, and alliga-

Co-owner Kathy Oleson at the counter of Boyett's Citrus Attraction.

tor wrestling. If you think you can get through and experience everything in an hour, think again. Allow for two or more hours.

Boyett's is a loving tribute to Florida's roadside-attraction heritage. You might come away with the feeling that it lacks a central theme because Boyett's pretty much covers the spectrum. But the central theme is simple: "Bring back great memories—or make new ones!" The place could use some signage, loaner maps, and work on a sidewalk that is a bit like a broken roller coaster, but this ain't Disney. Boyett's is a true mom-and-pop operation that allows for free creative expression, and there will certainly be more features added in the future!

MANATEE WATCHING

Crystal River is located on U.S. 19 along the Florida Gulf Coast about two hours north of Tampa and St. Petersburg. Several businesses offering manatee watching and snorkeling tours are located along the highway. The Three Sisters Springs Wildlife Refuge and Tours is located at 915 N. Suncoast Blvd., Crystal River, FL 34429; (352) 586-1170

Manatee watching at Crystal River is similar to tarpon feeding at Robbie's and bigger than ever before. It is advertised as the only place in the state where people can legally swim with manatees, although chasing or harassing them is illegal. The manatees are free to come and go, although during cold spells they are essentially trapped in the spring areas for warmth. That is why several small manatee sanctuaries have been established around King's Bay where humans are not allowed to enter. There are several tours to choose from in the Crystal River area, ranging from kayak tours to large diving/

Doug Alderson

Manatee watching is big business in places like Crystal River.

snorkeling boats. One can also take a trolley tour to the Three Sisters Springs National Wildlife Refuge on the edge of town and, from the vantage point of a boardwalk, view a stunning concentration of manatees seeking refuge during cold spells.

BIOLUMINESCENT TOURS

To learn more about the unique bioluminescent tours, contact A Day Away Kayak Tours in Titusville; (321) 268-2655

Manatee tour boat operators make a good living during the winter months, and, in that vein, ecotour companies are numerous throughout the Sunshine State, and new ones are born each year. Some guide people in kayaks and canoes or on foot trails and biking routes, while others utilize more mechanized means—airboats and swamp buggies. Private cattle ranchers with vast tracts of undeveloped land have seen ecotours as a way to augment income, while private kayak outfitters around Titusville have leaped on a seasonal phenomenon—bioluminescence. The best time to see the glowing dinoflagellates that create bioluminescence is after sunset from mid-July to mid-September, when the waters are warmest. Dip a paddle, witness a dolphin or manatee swim by, and the waters simply glow. It makes for a unique and memorable experience.

"FLORIDA'S MOST HAUNTED BRIDGE" AND OTHER GHOST TOURS

To take the haunted bridge tour, from U.S. 90 just east of Marianna, take County Road 166 north three miles. As the road curves right, turn left on Old U.S. Road. After four miles, turn left on County Road 162/ Jacob Road and proceed just over two miles to the parking area on the left near the bridge. Follow the trail south to Bellamy Bridge.

Another emerging nighttime activity in Florida is ghost tours. Their growing popularity can fall loosely under the heritage tourism umbrella, as they interpret history for those who wish to see or hear specters from the past. Rural Jackson County in the Panhandle features tours to a remote steel span over the Chipola River called the Bellamy Bridge—"Florida's most haunted bridge." To get there, you have to traverse a maze of back roads on the Bellamy Bridge Heritage Trail and then hike a half mile through an unspoiled floodplain forest. The site has been used as a crossing spot for centuries, and ghost stories abound.

St. Augustine may have made ghost tours famous, but many communities large and small have followed suit. These include Amelia Island, Tallahassee, Tampa, St. Petersburg, Orlando, Miami, Coconut Grove, Palm Beach, Fort Lauderdale, Kissimmee, St. Cloud, Sanford, Mount Dora, Bartow, Ocala, and Pensacola. Historic Monticello proudly calls itself "the South's most haunted small town." Downtown Tavares features a "Floating Ghosts Séance Tour" in which ghosts are called upon to reveal themselves, and the mediums of Cassadaga promise to speak to the dead.

Jackson County's historical Bellamy Bridge in the Panhandle is believed to be haunted.

Doug Alderson

St. Augustine's
Fort San Marcos
at night.

Doug Alderson

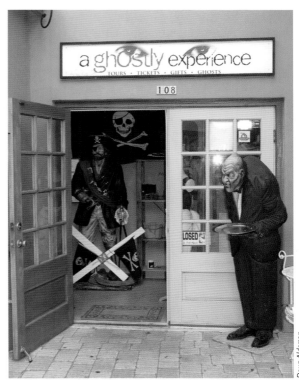
St. Augustine ghost tour headquarters.

Doug Alderson

POTTER'S WAX MUSEUM

Potter's Wax Museum is located in downtown St. Augustine on Orange Street at the corner of Cordova Street. It is situated two blocks west of South Castillo Drive and four blocks east of North Ponce de Leon Boulevard, the town's two main thoroughfares. Address: 31 Orange St., St. Augustine, FL 32084; (904) 829-9056

Whenever I see Potter's Wax Museum in St. Augustine—America's first—I flash back to an old *Twilight Zone* episode I viewed as a boy in which the wax figures come to life and cause a bit of mayhem. Obviously, this hasn't happened at Potter's because it has been a featured attraction since 1948, and it keeps up with the times by creating new life-size wax figures to portray contemporary celebrities, athletes, political figures, and fictional characters. Some of the figures don't need to come back to life because the original subjects are still alive! There are, also plenty of historical figures portrayed, ranging from early American presidents to Albert Einstein, making it a great family place to learn about history in a three-dimensional way. I was recently able to face my fears and live to tell about it, and you will, too.

SPOOK HILL

Spook Hill is marked by signs in Lake Wales off Highway 17/North Scenic Highway. Turn east onto J. A. Wiltshire Avenue East. Turn left at the dead end. The attraction sign is across the street from Spook Hill Elementary. Address: Fifth St., Lake Wales, FL 33853

Spook Hill is an oddity that's been around for decades. It is a small rise located in Lake Wales. You pull your car up to a white line, put it in neutral, and roll back while looking at the horizon to the right and left. The slopes of the adjoining countryside make you wonder why you would be rolling backward and not forward. It's an optical illusion from a simpler time, and it's free! A sign explains the legend of Spook Hill:

> Ages ago an Indian town on Lake Wales Lake was plagued with raids by a huge gator. The town's great warrior chief and the gator were killed in a final battle that created the huge swampy depression nearby. The chief was buried on its north side. Later, pioneer haulers coming from the old army trail atop the ridge above found their horses laboring there . . . at the foot of the ridge . . . and called it Spook Hill. Is it the gator seeking revenge, or the chief protecting his land?

The adjacent elementary school adopted the attraction's name and creatively adopted Casper the Friendly Ghost as its mascot.

A postcard from the late 1950s features Spook Hill in Lake Wales.

Ridge Distributing Company of Lakeland, Florida

THE LEGEND OF...

SPOOK HILL

AGES AGO AN INDIAN TOWN ON LAKE WAILES LAKE WAS PLAGUED
WITH RAIDS BY A HUGE GATOR. THE TOWN'S GREAT WARRIOR CHIEF AND
THE GATOR WERE KILLED IN A FINAL BATTLE THAT CREATED THE HUGE
SWAMPY DEPRESSION NEARBY. THE CHIEF WAS BURIED ON ITS NORTH SIDE
LATER PIONEER HAULERS COMING FROM THE OLD ARMY TRAIL ATOP THE
RIDGE ABOVE FOUND THEIR HORSES LABORING HERE... AT THE FOOT OF THE
RIDGE... AND CALLED IT SPOOK HILL.
IS IT THE GATOR SEEKING REVENGE, OR THE CHIEF PROTECTING HIS LAND?
**STOP CAR ON WHITE LINE, PLACE IN NEUTRAL,
AND LET IT ROLL BACK.**

The sign explaining the legend of Spook Hill.

Doug Alderson

SKUNK APE HEADQUARTERS

The Skunk Ape Headquarters is hard to miss. Take U.S. 41 (Tamiami Trail) to Ochopee in the Big Cypress National Preserve and look for it on the south side of the highway. Address: 40904 Tamiami Trail E., Ochopee, FL 34141; (239) 695-2275

Another Florida mystery may lurk in the deep recesses of the Florida Everglades and Big Cypress Swamp or perhaps in creative imaginations of the human mind. The skunk ape is Florida's version of Bigfoot, the Yeti, and the Abominable Snowman. With that said, who could drive past the Skunk Ape Headquarters in tiny Ochopee along the Tamiami Trail—near Florida's smallest post office—and not stop to check it out? You can learn all about the skunk ape's ideal habitat and diet (they love apples and lima beans) and how to bait a skunk ape (only on private lands, please). Adult male skunk apes can be seven feet tall and weigh more than 450 pounds, and they are very hairy! If seeing is not believing, the smell can be overwhelming—a strong aroma of rotten eggs or methane, since they may hide in alligator dens filled with animal carcasses and swamp gas, or they simply have an aversion to bathing. The research headquarters staff will even take the more serious visitor on excursions to search for skunk apes. So, as Ripley once said, believe it or not!

CORAL CASTLE

To find Coral Castle, take I-95 South to the Florida Turnpike South. Take the Florida Turnpike, past the Homestead Extension, to Exit 5/ Biscayne Drive (288th Street). Turn right, going west, onto Biscayne Drive. Continue for two miles and make a right turn onto SW 157th Avenue, where you'll see the Coral Castle entrance on the right. Address: 28655 S. Dixie Hwy., Homestead, FL 33033; (305) 248-6345

A true Florida mystery and unique treasure is the Coral Castle near Homestead on U.S. 1. One man of extremely small stature with a fourth-grade education, the late Edward Leedskainin, built a castle out of more than one thousand tons of coral rock as a tribute to his true, though unrequited, love. Engineers are puzzled as to how Leedskainin, using only hand tools, hoisted rocks weighing up to thirty tons into place, including perfectly balanced doors of solid rock, the largest weighing nine tons.

"I have discovered the secrets of the pyramids, and have found out how the Egyptians and the ancient builders in Peru, Yucatan, and Asia, with only primitive tools, raised and set in place blocks of stone weighing many tons!" said Leedskainin. But the builder failed to mention that those ancient societies often used thousands of slave laborers. His secret died with him. Speculation has ranged from levitation to UFOs. Leedskainin usually worked at night using a lantern, and few ever saw him work except for some nosy teens who claimed they saw him float blocks through the air. Regardless, it took Leedskainin from 1936 to 1951 to complete the castle. "A visit to the

Early brochure proclaiming the wonders of the Coral Castle.

Coral Castle is a rare treat for the most sophisticated traveler," states the brochure. And, as with many of Florida's oddities, that's no exaggeration!

EPILOGUE

◇◇◇◇◇◇◇◇◇◇◇◇◇◇◇◇◇◇

Admittedly, part of this journey has been a quest to recapture a childhood sense of wonderment and innocence. I yearned to feel the adventure of make-believe by suspending reality for a while, and I found it in the balletic arc of a Weeki Wachee mermaid, the iridescent depths of Silver Springs, and the squeals of delight I heard at Robbie's Tarpon Feeding.

In researching this book, I also found it fascinating to see the fork in Florida's tourism tree. While early tourists were largely content with fishing, hunting, sightseeing, and soaking in healing waters, extra features started to be added in the 1930s and 1940s to draw more visitors. Instead of just gazing into the blue portal of a clear spring, how about beautiful mermaids? Taking slow boat rides around a natural lake was good for some, but fabulous water-skiing shows appealed to the masses. Wild alligators are thrilling to see, but why not gaze upon concentrated numbers in big pits and pools . . . and have someone wrestle them! More year-round color was added to Florida's native landscapes with tropical plants from around the world. Throw in concrete dinosaurs, African animals, leaping dolphins, and a creative assortment of other accoutrements, and the Florida tourism scene is nearly complete.

The tourism branches have grown in many directions over time. Florida and its attractions can take you to many lands and worlds, or you can better appreciate the incredible beauty and biodiversity of all that is native and natural about this state. Both types of experiences are readily available, often only short distances apart. And even with tourism numbers exceeding one hundred million annually, most attractions retain a strong pulse available for all to discover.

A welcome addition is enhanced awareness of what has been coined ethical or sustainable tourism. "Responsible travel to natural areas that conserves the environment and improves the well-being of local people" is the mission of the Florida Society for Ethical Ecotourism. And the Destination Stewardship Center is dedicated to protecting "the world's distinctive places by supporting wisely managed tourism and enlightened destination stewardship." These efforts will help enable visitors to enjoy Florida's many attractions for generations to come.

BIBLIOGRAPHY

◇◇◇◇◇◇◇◇◇◇◇◇◇◇◇◇

"About LEGOLAND Florida." LEGOLAND. http://florida.legoland.com/en/EXPLORE-THE-PARK/About-Us/ (accessed July 30, 2014).

"About Monkey Jungle." Monkey Jungle. http://www.monkeyjungle.com/our-history (accessed June 7, 2015).

"About Us." Yearling Restaurant. http://www.yearlingrestaurant.net/about.html (accessed January 23, 2015).

Allen, Rick. "How Disney Brought Demise of Early Florida Theme Park." *Ocala Star-Banner*, January 5, 2011.

Barbour, George M. *Florida for Tourists, Invalids, and Settlers*. New York: D. Appleton and Company, 1882.

Bartram, William. *Travels through North and South Carolina, Georgia, East and West Florida*. Philadelphia: James and Johnson, 1776; New York: Dover, 1955.

Bok Tower Gardens. "Thomas Woltz, Landscape Architect & Storyteller." *Garden Path* (Spring 2014).

Bourget, Paul. *Outre-Mer: Impressions of America*. New York: Charles Scribner's Sons, 1895.

Brown, Robert H. "Floridaland." Florida's Lost Tourist Attractions. http://www.lostparks.com/fland.html (accessed August 6, 2014).

Brown, Tiara. "Everglades Wonder Gardens Granted $3.5 Million Loan from Bonita Springs." *Naples Herald*, March 21, 2015.

Citrus Tower. https://citrustower.com/ (accessed November 13, 2019).

Cook, David. "Ross Allen Leads Reptile Expeditions to South America." *Ocala Star-Banner*, May 5, 2013.

Corse, Carita Doggett. *Florida, Empire of the Sun*, comp. and ed. Bernal E. Clark. Tallahassee: Florida State Hotel Commission, 1930.

———. *Shrine of the Water Gods: Historical Account of Silver Springs*. St. Paul: Brown and Bigelow, 1944.

Dickinson, Joy Wallace. "Spring of Mermaids Goes Deep into Florida." *Orlando Sentinel*, August 17, 2003.

Douglas, Marjory Stoneman. *The Everglades: River of Grass*. Covington, GA: Mockingbird Books, 1975.

Dovell, J. E. *Florida: Historic, Dramatic, Contemporary*. Vol. 2. New York: Lewis Historical Publishing, 1952.

Draper, Robin. "Boyett's Citrus Attraction: Wacky and Wonderful." Authentic Florida, January 11, 2015. https://www.authenticflorida.com/articles/where-to-go/boyett-s-citrus-attraction-wacky-wonderful (accessed November 11, 2019).

"Fairchild Tropical Botanic Garden Mission and History." Fairchild Tropical Botanic Garden. https://www.fairchildgarden.org/About-Fairchild/Mission-History (accessed November 3, 2019).

Faris, John T. *Seeing the Sunny South*. Philadelphia: J. B. Lippincott, 1921.

Foster, John, Jr., and Sarah Whitmer Foster. *Calling Yankees to Florida: Harriet Beecher Stowe's Forgotten Tourist Articles*. Cocoa: Florida Historical Society Press, 2011.

"Four Freedoms Monument." Viva Florida. http://vivaflorida.org/Explore/Victory-Florida/WWII-Memorials-and-Sites-of-Interest/Four-Freedoms-Monument (accessed December 16, 2019).

Fox, Charles Donald. *The Truth about Florida*. New York: Charles Renard Corporation, 1925.

"Gatorland: From Tails to Tales." Gatorland. https://www.gatorland.com/historical-time-line (accessed November 13, 2019).

Genovese, Peter. *Roadside Florida: The Definitive Guide to the Kingdom of Kitsch*. Mechanicsburg, PA: Stackpole Books, 2006.

Glasgow, Vaughn L. *A Social History of the American Alligator*. New York: St. Martin's Press, 1991.

Glock, Allison. "The Gator Wrestlers." *Garden & Gun* (November 2008).

Grimes, David, and Tom Becnel. *Florida Curiosities*. 2nd ed. Guilford, CT: Insider's Guide, 2007.

Groff, Lauren. "Daughters of the Springs." *Oxford American* (Summer 2014): 41–48.

Hammond, John Martin. *Winter Journeys in the South*. Philadelphia and London: J. B. Lippincott Company, 1916.

Harper, Mark. "Water-Skiing Elephant Dies." *Daytona Beach News-Journal*, June 1, 2011.

Henshall, James A. *Camping and Cruising in Florida*. Port Salerno: Florida Classics Library, 1991. First published 1884.

Hinson, Mark. "Florida Sure Is a Strange Place to Meet Celebrities." *Tallahassee Democrat*, August 30, 2013.

"Historic Hotels in St. Pete/Clearwater." Visit St. Pete/Clearwater. http://www.visitstpeteclearwater.com/articles/historic-hotels-st-pete-clearwater-grande-dames (accessed August 6, 2014).

"History of Robbie's Marina." Robbie's of Islamorada. http://www.robbies.com/history-of-robbies.htm (accessed July 5, 2014).

Hollis, Tim. *Dixie before Disney: 100 Years of Roadside Fun*. Jackson: University Press of Mississippi, 1999.

———. *Glass Bottom Boats and Mermaid Tales*. Mechanicsburg, PA: Stackpole Books, 2006.

"Homosassa Springs State Park History." Florida State Parks. https://www.florida stateparks.org/parks-and-trails/ellie-schiller-homosassa-springs-wild life-state-park/history (accessed November 13, 2019).

Johnson, Neil. "Did Jimmy Buffett Boost Weeki Wachee Springs Park Attendance?" *Tampa Bay Times*, September 15, 2012.

Kilby, Rick. *Finding the Fountain of Youth: Ponce de León and Florida's Magical Waters.* Gainesville: University Press of Florida, 2013.

————. "Marine Studios: Undersea Innovation + Entertainment." *Old Florida: Ephemera and Musings from the State I'm In.* http://studiohourglass.blogspot .com/2010/02/marine-studios-undersea-innovation.html (accessed November 13, 2019).

Klinkenberg, Jeff. *Seasons of Real Florida.* Gainesville: University Press of Florida, 2004.

Landrum, Ney. *A Legacy of Green: The Making of Florida's Magnificent Park System.* N.p.: Florida Park Service Alumni Association, 2013.

Lanier, Sidney. *Florida: Its Scenery, Climate, and History.* Gainesville: University Press of Florida, 1976. Facsimile reproduction of 1875 edition.

"Lion Country Safari History." Lion Country Safari. http://www.lioncountrysafari.com/ information/history (accessed June 7, 2015).

Lyons, Ernest. *My Florida.* South Brunswick, NJ: A. S. Barnes and Company, 1969.

"Madison Four Freedoms Park." Madison County Florida Chamber of Commerce. http://madisonfl.org/parks.php (accessed December 16, 2019).

Magnini, Vincent P. "Florida Statewide Comprehensive Outdoor Recreation Plan Participation Study 2016–2017." Tallahassee, FL: Institute for Service Research, 2017.

"Marineland History Timeline." Marineland. http://marineland.net/wp-content/up-loads/2018/06/MDA_PressKit_June2018.pdf (accessed November 13, 2019).

Marsenberg, Theresa. "Paradise Lost: Florida's Segregated Beaches and Parks." The Florida Channel, September 29, 2014. http://thefloridachannel.org/videos/ florida-crossroads-shortcut-paradise-park (accessed December 23, 2014).

Mormino, Gary R. *Land of Sunshine, State of Dreams: A Social History of Modern Florida.* Gainesville: University Press of Florida, 2005.

Morris, Allen. *The Florida Handbook.* Tallahassee, FL: Peninsular Publishing, 1953.

Nash, Ranger Mike. "An Audiotaped Interview with Ricou Browning." Wakulla Springs State Park "Creaturefest," November 5, 2003. Oral History Transcript, Florida Park Service Archives, Tallahassee.

Nornabell, Major H. M. *The Sanctuary and Singing Tower.* New York: Charles Francis Press, 1929.

O'Brien, William. "The Strange Career of a Florida State Park: Uncovering a Jim Crow Past." *Historical Geography* 35 (2007): 160–84.

"Park Endorsed by Movie Icon." *Space Coast Daily*, September 12, 2013.

Pennekamp, John D. "Playground for All the People." *Florida Highways* (January 1951).

Proby, Kathryn Hall. *Audubon in Florida*. Coral Gables, FL: University of Miami Press, 1974.

"Rambler." *Guide to Florida*. Gainesville: University Press of Florida, 1964. Facsimile reproduction of the 1875 edition.

"Ravine Gardens State Park History." Ravine Gardens State Park. https://www .floridastateparks.org/parks-and-trails/ravine-gardens-state-park/history (accessed October 31, 2019).

Rawlings, Marjorie Kinnan. *Cross Creek*. New York: Charles Scribner's Sons, 1942.

Revels, Tracy J. *Sunshine Paradise: A History of Florida Tourism*. Gainesville: University Press of Florida, 2011.

Riley, Ruth J. *Memories of Rainbow Springs*. Dunnellon, FL: Fruit Tree Press, 1995.

Rinhart, Floyd, and Marion Rinhart. *Victorian Florida: America's Last Frontier*. Atlanta: Peachtree Publishers, 1986.

Robichaud, William F. *Survival Safari: Cross-country from the Atlantic to Gulf of Mexico*. Silver Springs, FL: Ross Allen's Reptile Institute, 1962.

"Sarasota Jungle Gardens History." Sarasota Jungle Gardens. https://sarasotajungle gardens.com/about-us (accessed November 13, 2019).

Schensul, Jill. "In Old Florida, Weeki Wachee and Other Early Tourist Attractions Still Kicking." *Orlando Sentinel*, March 8, 2011.

Scoggin, Lewis G. "Park Service Briefs." Florida Park Service News, September 1947.

"See and Do It All at Floridaland!" *Florida Memory Blog*. https://www.floridamemory .com/blog/2014/09/22/see-and-do-it-all-at-floridaland (accessed November 13, 2019).

"Shell Factory & Nature Park." Shell Factory & Nature Park. https://www.shellfactory .com/about.php (accessed February 10, 2016).

"Silver Springs State Park near Ocala Opens." Associated Press, October 1, 2013.

"Skunk Ape Headquarters." Skunk Ape Research Center. http://www.skunkape.biz (accessed January 26, 2015).

Smiley, Nixon. *Florida: Land of Images*. Miami: E. A. Seemann Publishing, 1972.

Smith, Mark. "Floridaland Had 'Everything under the Sun.'" Sarasota History Center. http://www.sarasotahistoryalive.com/stories/journals-of-yesteryear/florida land-had-everything-under-the-sun (accessed August 6, 2014).

Smith, Rick, dir. *Patrick Smith's Florida: A Sense of Place*. Cambria, CA: Panorama Studios, 2005.

"Solomon's Castle." http://www.roadsideamerica.com/story/2059 (accessed January 26, 2015).

"Solomon's Castle." http://www.solomonscastle.org (accessed January 26, 2015).

Solomon, Peggy Reilly. *The Castle in the Swamp: The Story of Solomon's Castle*. Ona, FL: Little Silver Books, 2009.

St. Petersburg Area Chamber of Commerce. *St. Petersburg and Pinellas County: The Gulf Coast Jewel on Tampa Bay.* St. Petersburg, FL: R. R. Donnelly & Sons, 2000.

Starck, Walter. "Robbie's of Islamorada, a Florida Keys Institution." FlyLifeMagazine .com, January 17, 2014. http://flylifemagazine.com/of-interest-robbies-of-isla morada-a-florida-keys-institution (accessed July 5, 2014).

"The St. Augustine Alligator Farm Zoological Park: A Story More Than 100 Years in the Making." St. Augustine Alligator Farm. http://www.alligatorfarm.com/history .html (accessed December 26, 2014).

Stevenson, Jim A. *My Journey in Florida's State Parks: A Naturalist's Memoir.* Tallahassee, FL: Self-published, 2013.

"Tarpon Springs." Spongeorama. http://spongeoramacruiselines.com/tarpon-springs (accessed February 11, 2016).

Thorner, James. "Faded Roadside Attraction Dupree Gardens to Vanish." *St. Petersburg Times*, September 6, 2002.

"Tower & Gardens—Our History." Bok Tower Gardens. http://boktowergardens.org/ tower-gardens/our-history (accessed July 29, 2014).

Treister, Kenneth, and David Price. *Bok Tower Gardens: America's Taj Mahal.* New York: Rizzoli International, 2013.

Valentine, Danny. "Roof at Weeki Wachee Mermaid Theater to Be Returned to Its Original Look." *Tampa Bay Times*, July 9, 2014.

"Venetian Pool." Super Coral Gables. https://www.coralgables.com/departments/ CommunityRecreation/venetian-pool (accessed August 27, 2019).

Vickers, Lu. *Cypress Gardens: America's Tropical Wonderland.* Gainesville: University Press of Florida, 2010.

Vickers, Lu, and Sara Dionne. *Weeki Wachee: City of Mermaids.* Gainesville: University Press of Florida, 2007.

"Visit." The Ringling. https://www.ringling.org/visit (accessed February 11, 2016).

"Washington Oaks Gardens State Park History." Washington Oaks Gardens State Park. https://www.floridastateparks.org/parks-and-trails/washington-oaks-gar dens-state-park/history (accessed October 31, 2019).

"Webb's City." Florida's Lost Tourist Attractions. http://www.lostparks.com/webbs .html (accessed August 2, 2014).

Werndli, Phil. *Florida State Parks . . . 75 Years.* Altamonte Springs: Florida Media, 2010.

"What to See at Edison Ford." Edison & Ford Winter Estates. http://www.edisonford winterestates.org/about/what-youll-see (accessed February 10, 2016).

White, Dale. "Doctor Wants to Bring Medical Tourism to Springs." *Sarasota Herald-Tribune*, April 12, 2013.

White, J. W. *White's Guide to Florida and Her Famous Resorts.* Jacksonville, FL: Dacosta Publishing, 1890.

Winter, Nevin O. *Florida: The Land of Enchantment.* Boston: Page Company, 1918.

Wood, Barbara Lindner. *North from Ocala*. Ocala, FL: Special Publications, 2000.

Works Progress Administration. *Florida: A Guide to the Southernmost State*. New York: Oxford University Press, 1939.

Wynne, Nick. *The Tin Can Tourists in Florida, 1900–1970*. Charleston, SC: Arcadia Publishing, 1999.

Interviews

Bruegger, John. Personal communication. St. Augustine Alligator Farm Zoological Park, 2015.

D'hollander, Geert. Personal meeting. Bok Tower Gardens, 2014.

Dane, Liz. Personal telephone communication about De Leon Springs history, 2015.

Darlington, Jim. Personal meeting. St. Augustine Alligator Farm Zoological Park, 2015.

Gavin, Don. Personal meeting. Wakulla Springs, 2013.

Gernert, Bob. Personal communication. LEGOLAND/Cypress Gardens, 2014.

Hart, Bill. Personal communication. Canton, Ohio, 2014.

Hileman, Mike. Personal meeting. Gatorland, 2010.

May, Melody. Personal meeting. Tallahassee, 2014.

McGinnis, Terran. Personal meeting. Marineland, 2015.

Oleson, Kathy. Personal meeting. Boyett's Citrus Attraction, 2019.

Ososky, Brian. Personal meeting. Bok Tower Gardens, 2014.

Padgett, Audrey. Personal meeting. LEGOLAND/Cypress Gardens, 2014.

Price, David. Personal meeting. Bok Tower Gardens, 2014.

Rebillot, Susan. Personal communication. Sunken Gardens, 2015.

Register, Patty. Personal communication. Gatorama, 2014.

Royle, Phil. Personal meeting. LEGOLAND/Cypress Gardens, 2014.

Rusing, Marj. Personal telephone communication about De Leon Springs history, 2015.

Sierra-Valentin, Esther. Personal communication. Lion Country Safari, 2015.

Solomon, Howard. Personal meeting. Solomon's Castle, 2015.

Solomon, Peggy. Personal meeting. Solomon's Castle, 2015.

INDEX

◇◇◇◇◇◇◇◇◇◇◇◇◇◇◇◇◇

ABOUT THE AUTHOR

◇◇◇◇◇◇◇◇◇◇◇◇◇◇◇

Doug Alderson furthers his lifelong love for classic Florida in this second edition of his popular guide, one in which he adds several new attractions and both vintage and contemporary photos. His first edition was honored by the Florida Writers Association as one of the top five published books of 2017. He has also won four first-place Royal Palm Literary Awards for travel books and several other state and national writing and photography awards.

Alderson's other books include *America's Alligator: A Popular History of Our Most Celebrated Reptile*, *Wild Florida Waters*, *The Great Florida Seminole Trail*, *Waters Less Traveled*, *New Dawn for the Kissimmee River*, *Encounters with Florida's Endangered Wildlife*, and *Spooky Stories from the Swamp: Tales from the Florida Back Country*. Additionally, his articles and photographs have been featured in magazines such as *Sea Kayaker*, *Wildlife Conservation*, *Native Peoples*, *American Forests*, *Sierra*, *Mother Earth News*, and *A.T. Journeys*. He is also an adventurer, having hiked the entire Appalachian Trail, coordinated a group walk across the United States, backpacked through Europe, and mapped a 1,500-mile sea-kayaking trail around Florida. He received the inaugural Environmental Service Award by Paddle Florida in 2015 "for conspicuous commitment, unflagging dedication and love of Florida's natural environment." For more information, visit www.dougalderson.net.

Underwater thanksgiving at Rainbow Springs taken by Harvey Slade in 1953.

Courtesy of Florida Archives